THE EVALUATOR
2ND EDITION

COPYRIGHT MARK GERECHT

All Rights Reserved

2002
Distributed by:

Byrrd Enterprises, Inc.
1302 Lafayette Drive
Alexandria, Virginia 22308
1-800-628-0901
Fax: 1-703-768-4086
Email: Byrrdbooks@AOL.Com

BOOKS / CD AVAILABLE FROM

MARK GERECHT

THE MENTOR

**Everything You Need To Know About
Leadership And Counseling**

THE TRAINER

A Training Guide For All Ranks

THE EVALUATOR

**The Comprehensive Guide For Preparing
NCOER Counselings and Evaluation Reports**

THE WRITER

The Comprehensive Guide For Writing Awards

TOOLS OF THE TRADE (CD FORMAT)

Leadership Resources Volume 1

THE EVALUATOR

PROLOGUE

The purpose of this book is to assist soldiers/leaders in preparing evaluation reports and conducting NCOER counseling, and to provide information on other areas relating to the Noncommissioned Officer Evaluation System. A majority of the bullet comments have been extracted from the NCOER Update. Therefore these bullets have been chosen by members of the promotion board to embody the characteristics of what board members expect in a bullet comment. You will find samples of bullets relating to excellence, success, needs improvement, senior rater comments, and values. I hope that this **guide** will assist you in preparing evaluations and counselings for the soldiers you lead.

Evaluation reports are perhaps the most important document in a soldier's career. Therefore it is imperative that you as a leader prepare a fair, just, and accurate report. As a leader you have a duty and responsibility to conduct solid performance counseling that helps develop the soldier and identifies areas that need improvement. Ensure that your counseling encompasses all areas that may affect a soldier: standards, duties, responsibilities, additional duties, areas of emphasis, education, equal opportunity, off-duty employment, suggestions on how to correct substandard areas, and that counseling concludes with the soldier reviewing a working copy of the NCOER. This ensures that there are no surprises when the actual NCOER is submitted. In addition I suggest that you read AR 623-205, and contact your local S-1 or PSB if you have any questions.

Please keep in mind that these are my personal opinions and not the views of the United States Army. My intent is to inform soldiers and to discuss the ideas and methods that I have discovered along the way, hoping that this will assist other soldiers and leaders . I hope you will find this book useful. I encourage your comments and suggestions.

THE EVALUATOR

THIS BOOK IS DEDICATED TO:

My Lovely Wife Patty,

Our Daughter Shania Ann,

My Loving Parents,

All the Soldiers With Whom I Have Had the Honor to Serve

&

FINALLY, TO THE PUBLISHER FOR WORKING WITH ME AND GIVING ME THE OPPORTUNITY TO PRODUCE THIS BOOK.

EDITED BY DEBORAH SHEPHERD

THE EVALUATOR

TABLE OF CONTENTS

PAGE

CHAPTER 1: THE NCOER SYSTEM   13

Introduction   14
An Overview of AR 623-205 (Key Points to Remember)   15
    Commander's Responsibility   15
    Standards of Service   15
    Performance Evaluation   16
    Potential Evaluation   16
    Commander's Inquiry   16
    Designating a Rater   19
    Rater Responsibilities   20
    Designating a Senior Rater   21
    Senior Rater Responsibilities   21
    Designating a Reviewer   22
    Reviewer Responsibilities   23
    Loss of Rating Chain Official   23
    Counseling Requirements   24
    Administrative Data   25
    Duty Description   25
    Rules for Bullet Statements   26
    Prohibited Narrative Gimmicks   26
    APFT Entry   27
    HT/WT Entry   28
    Overall Performance & Potential   28
    Senior Rater Narrative Rules   29
    Stand Alone Reports   29
    Unproven Derogatory Information   30
    Prohibited Comments   31
    Comments Concerning Marital Status   31
    Alcohol and Drug Abuse Program   32
    Performance as an Equal Opportunity NCO   33
    Types of Reports   33
    Report Codes By Type   38
    Summary   38

CHAPTER 2: PREPARING THE NCOER FROM START TO FINISH   39

    Prior to the Initial Counseling   41
    Sample: DA Form 2166-8-1 (NCOER Checklist)   46
    Sample: Filling out the DA Form 2166-8 (NCOER-Front)   47

THE EVALUATOR

	PAGE
Sample: Filling out the DA Form 2166-8 (NCOER-Back)	48
DA Form 2166-8 by the Numbers (Block by Block explanation)	49
NCOER Counseling Checklist	51
CHAPTER 3: BULLET COMMENTS	53
Value Bullets	54
Loyalty	54
Duty	55
Respect	56
Selfless-Service	57
Honor	59
Integrity	59
Personal Courage	60
Competence Bullets of Excellence	62
Awards	62
Basic Skills	63
Competition	63
Deployment	64
Development	65
Dollars & Percentages	68
Education	70
Inspections	71
Maintenance	72
Recognition	72
Retention	74
Weapons	75
Works Above Grade or Selected Over Others	75
Miscellaneous	76
Competence Bullets of Success	78
Competition	78
Deployment	78
Development	78
Dollars & Percentages	79
Education	79
Inspections	80
Maintenance	80
Recognition	80
Weapons	81

THE EVALUATOR

		PAGE
Works Above Grade or Selected Over Others		81
Miscellaneous		82
Competence Bullets Needs Improvement		83
Physical Fitness & Bearing Bullets of Excellence		85
Individual Achievement		85
Group Achievement		86
Physical Fitness & Bearing Bullets of Success		87
Individual Achievement		87
Group Achievement		88
Physical Fitness & Bearing Bullets Needs Improvement		89
APFT		89
Appearance		90
Weight Control		90
Leadership Bullets of Excellence		91
Awards		91
Basic Skills		91
Competition		92
Deployment		94
Development		95
Dollars & Percentages		95
Education		96
Inspections		96
Maintenance		96
Recognition		96
Retention		98
Weapons		98
Works Above Grade or Selected Over Others		99
Miscellaneous		100
Leadership Bullets of Success		101
Competition		101
Deployment		101
Development		102

THE EVALUATOR

	PAGE
Dollars & Percentages	102
Education	102
Inspections	103
Maintenance	103
Recognition	103
Weapons	103
Works Above Grade or Selected Over Others	104
Miscellaneous	104
Leadership Bullets Needs Improvement	105
Training Bullets of Excellence	108
APFT	108
Awards	108
Basic Skills	109
Competition	109
Deployment	110
Development	110
Dollars & Percentages	112
Education	112
Inspections	113
Maintenance	113
Recognition	113
Retention	114
Weapons	114
Miscellaneous	115
Training Bullets of Success	116
Basic Skills	116
Competition	116
Deployment	116
Development	117
Education	117
Inspections	117
Maintenance	118
Recognition	118
Weapons	118
Miscellaneous	118
Training Bullets Needs Improvement	120

THE EVALUATOR

	PAGE
Responsibility Bullets of Excellence	121
Awards	121
Competition	121
Deployment	121
Dollars & Percentages	122
Inspections	124
Maintenance	125
Recognition	125
Safety	126
Works Above Grade or Selected Over Others	126
Miscellaneous	127
Responsibility Bullets of Success	127
Deployment	127
Development	127
Dollars & Percentages	128
Inspections	128
Maintenance	128
Safety	128
Works Above Grade or Selected Over Others	129
Miscellaneous	129
Responsibility Bullets Needs Improvement	129
Senior Rater Potential Bullet Examples (Strong Bullets)	131
Senior Rater Potential Bullet Examples (Fully Capable or Needs Improvement)	136
CHAPTER 4: NCOER APPEALS	138
Commander's Inquiry	139
Appeals Process	139
Army Board of Military Records	139
Overview of the Appeals Process	140
Items to Consider	143
Preparing for the Appeal	143
NCOER Appeal Checklist	145
Sample Request for Commander's Inquiry	146

THE EVALUATOR

                                                                PAGE

Summary   148

CHAPTER 5: RELIEF FOR CAUSE (Suggestions)   149

    Introduction   150
    Definition   151
    Counseling   152
    Cases of Inefficiency or Unacceptable Duty Performance 154
    Cases of Misconduct or Willful Neglect 156
    Actions After Relief   156
    Items to Consider During Relief for Cause 158

CHAPTER 6: NCOER FREQUENTLY ASKED QUESTIONS   160

    Visually Centering Bullet Comments   161
    Changes to an NCOER After Submission (Inconsistencies) 161
    Duty MOS vs. Individuals MOS   161
    Appeals Process   162
    Maintaining Previous NCOER's From a Different Rater 162
    Senior Rater Comment Guidance   163
    APFT Scores   164
    Civilians Rating NCO's   164
    DUI Offense   164
    PSB Request a Copy of MMRB to Support Profile 165
    NCOER with Incorrect Correct Rating Chain 165
    Suspension Pending Investigation (Relief for Cause) 165
    Using Quotas for Among the Best and 1/1 Ratings 166
    4 Digit Thru Date on the 2166-8   166
    Downloading the DA 2166-8 and 2166-8-1 166
    Being Assigned Below Your Rank   167
    Referencing An Allegation   167
    Can a Junior NCO's Rate an NCO of the Same Rank 167
    Retirement and Transition leave NCOER's 168
    Profiles and APFT Scores   168
    When a Rater is Relieved   168
    NCO's that Reenlist for the College Option How Are They Rated 168
    Can a Junior CSM Rate a Senior SGM   169
    Handwritten or Computer Generated "X"'s 169
    **Does the Word Potential Have to Appear in the Senior
        Rater's Comments** 170
    Conditional Promotion to SGT & Then Administratively Reduced 170
    Dating the Blocks on the NCOER   170

  PAGE

Proper Characters for MOS (O vs 0)   171
Reviewer Has PCS'd Without Signing the Report   171
What Score on the APFT Constitutes an Excellence   172
Comments Concerning Community Activities   172
Within Body Fat Standards Comment   172
NCO That is Overweight, Does not Meet Body Fat Standards
        but has a Medical Condition   172
NCO Fails APFT and Get a Profile Preventing a Retest   173
Bullets Past or Present Tense   173
Can a SFC rate a SSG in an SFC Position   173
MSG rating a GS-13   174
Soldier on Profile and Unable to take APFT   174
P3 Profile Prohibits taking the APFT   174
NCO in the Overweight Program Does not Meet Body Fat
        Standards but is Making Progress   175
Comments Concerning Areas of Special Emphasis or Appointed
        Duties   175
Commander's Inquiry   175
Clarification of Changes   176
Signature Dates   177
NCO' working in Officer Positions   178
Excellence Ratings for Physical Fitness & Military Bearing   178
Senior Rater Comments of Potential   178
Website Guidance- Is it Official   178

CHAPTER 7: WORD LISTING   180

Adjectives   181
Verbs   185
Nouns   186

THE EVALUATOR

The author encourages and welcomes comments, suggestions, ideas, or questions sent to:

MENTORPUBS1@AOL.COM

All material will be reviewed for possible use in future printings. Please provide your address and phone number with your correspondence.

In this book when we use the term **"commander"** it refers to commanders at all levels. Some commanders have different types of authority. The local policy on the authority of a commander should be checked in your area. In addition, any reference to the term **"he"** should be understood to include both genders.

CHAPTER ONE

THE NCOER SYSTEM

Note: Keep in mind this is an overview of the regulation. Prior to making any decision consult the regulation. DO NOT use this guide as a basis for your decisions.

THE EVALUATOR

THE NCOER SYSTEM

Publications for Review:

- AR 623-205   Noncommissioned Officer Evaluation Reporting System
- AR 600-20   Army Command Policy
- AR 600-9   Army Weight Control Program
- AR 600-37   Letters of Reprimand
- AR 350-41   Training in Units
- AR 27-10   Military Justice
- FM 22-100   Leadership
- FM 22-101   Counseling

Local Items for Possible Review:

- **Local Policy Letters**
- **MACOM Directives**
- **Supplements to ARs**
- **NCOER Updates**

Possible Web Sites for Review:

- **PERSCOM ONLINE: www.perscom.army.mil**

- **Army Counseling Web site: www.counseling.army.mil**

- **Enlisted Records and Evaluation Center: www.erec.army.mil**

Introduction

Army Regulation 623-205 is the primary source relating to the Noncommissioned Officer Evaluation Report. If you have any questions concerning the NCOER this should be your initial starting point. If you are unable to resolve your question contact one of the following individuals: S-1, PSB, IG, or JAG. These individuals should be able to point you in the right direction or provide you with the answer to your question. **Remember, the items identified in this book are not to be used as the authority for action. The authority for action is the regulation and/or local policy.**

THE EVALUATOR

<u>An Overview of AR 623-205 (Key Points to Remember)</u>

Commanders are Responsible for Ensuring (para. 1-4b):

- A copy of the regulation is available for the rated NCO and the rating officials. (1-4b(1)(a)

- Rating chains correspond as nearly as practical to the chain of command and supervision within an organization, regardless of component or geographical location. (1-4b(1)(b))

- Rating chains are drawn up by name, given effective dates, published, and distributed to each rated NCO and each member of the rating chain. Any changes to rating chains will also be published and distributed. No changes may be retroactive. Also see Rating Chain (para. 1-4b(1)(c) and 1-12).

- Rating officials give timely counseling to subordinates on professionalism and job performance, encouraging self-improvement when needed. (1-4f)

- Reports are prepared by the rating officials designated in the published rating scheme. (1-4g)

- The duties in para. 6-3 (Commander's Inquiry) are performed when a report appears to be illegal, unjust, or otherwise in violation of this regulation. (1-4k)

Standards of Service (para. 1-11):

- The rater will be senior to the rated NCO; the senior rater will be senior to the rater; and the reviewer will be senior to the senior rater. (1-11b(3))

THE EVALUATOR

- Mandatory evaluations will normally cover a minimum of 90 days. (1-11b(4))

Rating Chain Performance and Potential Evaluations (para. 1-13 and Chapter 2):

Performance Evaluation:

- Performance evaluations are assessments on how well the NCO met duty requirements and adhered to professional standards of the NCO Corps. Performance is evaluated by observing action and demonstrated behavior, and results from the point of view of the values and NCO responsibilities identified in para. 3-10. When evaluating performance consider the following: (1-13a)

    o Relative experience of the NCO. (1-13a(1))
    o Efforts made by the NCO. (1-13a(2))
    o Results that could be reasonably expected given the time and resources available. (1-13a(3))

Potential Evaluation: (1-13b)

- Potential evaluations are performance-based assessments of the rated NCO's ability, compared with that of NCOs of the same grade, to perform in positions of greater responsibility and/or higher grade. Assessment of potential applies to all NCOs regardless of their opportunity to be selected for higher positions or grades, and ignores such factors as impending retirements or release from active duty.

Commander's Inquiry (para. 1-15 and 6-3)

Note: The Commander's Inquiry will be discussed in more detail in Chapter 4 of this book.

THE EVALUATOR

- The purpose of the inquiry is to look into alleged errors, injustices, and illegalities in NCOERs (para. 6-3).

- The primary purpose of the Commander's Inquiry is to provide a greater degree of command involvement in preventing obvious injustices to the rated NCO and to correct errors before they become a matter of permanent record (para. 6-3).

- A secondary purpose is to obtain command involvement in clarifying errors or injustices after the evaluation report is accepted at USAEREC, CNBG, State Adjutant General's officer or AR PERSCOM (para. 6-3).

- The report will be made by a commander (major or above) in the chain of command above the designated rating official involved in the allegation (para. 6-4).

- Commanders may appoint an officer, senior to the designate rating officials involved in the allegation, to make the inquiry (para. 6-4).

- If the report has already been forwarded to and accepted at USAEREC, CNBG, State Adjutant General's officer, or ARPERSCOM, the inquiry must be conducted by either the commander who is still in the command position at the time the report was rendered, or by a subsequent commander in the position. However, the report must be forwarded not later than 120 days after the "THRU" date of the report (para. 6-4).

- The provisions of AR 15-6 do not normally apply to inquiries; however, commanders may determine that the provisions of AR 15-6 apply (para. 6-3).

- The rated NCO or anyone having knowledge of the alleged illegality, injustice, or violation may bring such matters to the commander's attention (para. 6-3).

- When it is brought to the attention of the commander that a report may be unjust, illegal, or in violation of the regulation, the commander will look into the allegation(para. 1-15).

THE EVALUATOR

- The inquiry will be confined to matters relating to the clarity of the report, the facts contained in the report, the compliance of the report with the regulation, and the conduct of the rated NCO and rating officials (para. 1-15).

- Inquiry may be as formal or informal as the commander deems appropriate (para. 6-4(3)b).

- Will not be used to document differences of opinion between the rating officials or commander about an NCO's performance and potential (para. 6-4a).

- The commander may find that the report contains serious irregularities or errors. Examples may include: (para. 6-4a)

  - Improperly designated or unqualified rating officials. (6-4a(1))
  - Inaccurate or untrue statements. (6-4a(2))
  - Lack of objectivity or fairness by rating officials. (6-4a(3))

- The commander will not pressure or force rating officials to change their evaluation (para.6-4c).

- The commander may not evaluate the rated NCO as a substitute for, or in addition to, the designated rating officials (para. 6-4d).

- The commander will not use the Commander Inquiry provisions to forward information derogatory to the rated NCO (para. 6-4e).

- The Commander's Inquiry will include: findings, recommendations, and conclusions in a format that can be filed with the NCOER in the soldier's OMPF (6-4g).

THE EVALUATOR

Rules for Designating the Rater (para. 2-4)a: The rater must be:

- The immediate supervisor of the NCO. (2-4a(1))

- Designated as the rater for a minimum of 90 days (see paras. 3-30, 3-32, 3-33, 4-12, and 5-12 for exceptions). (2-4a(1))

- A sergeant or higher, and senior to the rated NCO by pay grade of date or rank. (2-4a(2))

- If an NCO is on a promotion list for E-7, E-8, or E-9 and serving in an authorized position for the new grade, they may rate the NCO if, after promotion the rater will be senior in grade or date of rank. Then he may rate the NCOs he supervises. (2-4a(2))

- A 1SG, SGM, or CSM frocked may rate any NCO under his supervision if after promotion the rated NCO will be senior to the rated soldier by pay grade or date of rank. (2-4a(2))

- GS-6 and above may be designated by the commander as a rater when military supervisors are not available and when the civilian supervisor is in the best position to accurately evaluate the NCO's performance. (2-4b)

- Members of allied forces are not authorized to be raters. (2-4d)

- Members of other U.S. military services who meet the qualifications may be raters. (2-4c)

- May act as both rater and senior rater when the rater is a general officer. (2-4f)

THE EVALUATOR

Rater Responsibilities (para. 2-9):

- Counsel the rated NCO on duty performance and professional development. (2-9a)

- Discuss and define duty description. (2-9a)

- Counsel corporals and sergeants within the first 30 days of the effective date of promotion. (2-9a)

- Assess the performance of the rated NCO, using all reasonable means. (2-9c)

- Prepare a fair, correct report evaluating the NCO's duty performance, values/responsibilities, and potential. (2-9d)

- Verify parts I and II, enter the Army Physical Fitness Test and height and weight entries for part IVc. (2-9e)

- Date and enter his/her signature in part IIa. (2-9f)

- The DA Form 2166-8-1 is mandatory for use by the rater when counseling all NCOs. (2-9a)

- Prepare a working copy of the NCOER to be used in conjunction with the DA Form 2166-8-1.

- The DA Form 2166-8-1 will be maintained until the evaluation report has been approved and submitted to USAEREC on sergeants and above. It will be maintained on corporals for one year. There is no regulatory guidance to keep the DA Form 2166-8-1 beyond this timeframe; however it may be appropriate to keep it to support possible personnel actions in the future. (2-9b)

THE EVALUATOR

Rules for Designating the Senior Rater (para. 2-5): The senior rater must be:

- In the direct line of supervision of the rated NCO. (2-5a(1))

- Designated as the senior rater for a minimum of 60 days (see paras. 3-30, 4-12, and 5-11 for exceptions). (2-5a(1))

- Senior to the rater by either pay grade or date of rank. (2-5a(2))

- May be a GS-6 when military personnel are not available. (2-5b)

- Members of other U.S. military services may be senior raters if they meet the requirements listed above. (2-5c)

- Members of Allied military forces are not authorized to be raters. (2-5d)

- May act as both rater and senior rater when the rater is a general officer. (2-5e)

Senior Rater Responsibilities (para. 2-11):

- Use a reasonable means to become familiar with the rated NCO's performance. (2-11a)
- Prepare, a fair, correct report; evaluating duty performance, professionalism and potential (2-11b)

- Date and enter his/her signature in part II b. (2-11c)

- Obtain the rated NCO's signature in part II of the NCOER. (2-11d)

- Ensure that the rated NCO understands that his signature does not constitute agreement or disagreement with the evaluation. The signature means that the rated

THE EVALUATOR

NCO has seen the completed report and has verified the administrative data, the rating officials are proper, the duty description is accurate, and includes counseling dates. (2-11d)

- If counseling dates are omitted the senior rater will enter a statement explaining why in part Ve. (2-11d)

- Enter appropriate statement "NCO refuses to sign" or "NCO is not available for signature." (2-11d)

- Ensure bullets support appropriate ratings in part IV b-f. (2-11e)

- Ensure that the statement "Senior rater does not meet minimum qualifications" is entered in part Ve (if this comment is appropriate). (2-11f)

- Not render an evaluation in part Vc or d when the minimum time requirements are not met. (2-11g)

- Sign part IId when also serving as the reviewer. (2-11h)

- Not direct that the rater change an evaluation that he or she believes to be honest. (2-11i)

Rules for Designating the Reviewer (para. 2-6):

- Must be a commissioned officer, warrant officer, command sergeant major, or sergeant major in the direct line of supervision. (2-6a)

- Must be senior in grade or date of rank. (2-6a)

- No minimum time period is required for the reviewer. (2-6b)

THE EVALUATOR

- GS-9 and above may act as a reviewer when the grade and line of supervision requirements are met, either the rater or senior rater is a uniformed Army official. If rater or senior rater are other than uniformed Army rating officials described in para 2-6f and no uniform Army reviewer is available the report will be reviewed by a uniformed Army officer in the rated NCOs PSB or unit administrative office (2-6 c-d)

- Members of Allied forces are not authorized to be reviewers. (2-6 e)

- When the rater or senior rater is a general officer that official may also act as the reviewer. (2-6f)

Reviewer Responsibilities (para. 2-13): The reviewer will:

- Ensure that the proper rater and senior rater complete the report. (2-13a)

- Examine the evaluations of the rater and senior rater and ensure that they are clear, consistent, and just in accordance with the facts. (2-13b)

- Indicate concurrence or nonoccurrence with the rater and or senior rater by marking the appropriate block. (2-13c)

- When the nonoccurrence block is marked, prepare an enclosure not to exceed one page (see Fig. 3-8).

- Consult with rating chain concerning any discrepancies. (2-13c)

- The reviewer may not direct the rating chain to change an evaluation they believe to be honest.

Loss of a Rating Chain Official (paras. 2-14 and 2-15):

THE EVALUATOR

- If either the senior rater or reviewer are removed it is treated as a routine change and a new rating official is designated. The new senior rater or reviewer may participate in the evaluation report once the minimum requirements have been met.

- When the rater is removed: (2-15c)

    o If the minimum period (90 days) has not been met, then the period is nonrated and a new rater is designated.

    o If the minimum period (90 days) has been met, the senior rater will perform the rater's function, provided rater qualifications are met. The senior rater serves as both the rater and senior rater.

    o When the senior rater acts as the rater, the rated period of the report will be the period the senior rater has been in the chain.

    o When the rater is suspended, the suspended time will be counted as non-rated time. (2-15b)

- When a rating official is relieved, reduced, AWOL, or incapacitated he will not be permitted to evaluate his subordinates. (2-14)

Counseling Requirements (paras. 3-4 and 3-5):

- Face-to-face counseling is mandatory (para. 3-5c).

- Initial counseling will be accomplished within the first 30 days of the rating period. (3-5c)
    o Initial counseling's primary focus is on communicating performance standards to the rated NCO.

THE EVALUATOR

- o Let the NCO know what is expected during the rating period
- o Discuss rating chain, duty description, values/responsibilities, standards for success.

- The Army has identified special areas of interests that include (para. 3-5d):
  - o Civilian position management (AR 690-500)
  - o Internal Control System (AR 11-2)
  - o Audits (AR 36-2)
  - o Safety (AR 385-10)
  - o Contracting and Acquisition (DODD 5000.52-M)
  - o Information Security Program (AR 380-19)
  - o Property Accountability (Supply Update)
  - o Personnel Management Responsibility for Army Civilians (AR 10-20)

- Conducted at least quarterly (every 3 months) (3-5c(2))
  - o Primary focus on how well the NCO is doing, updating duty description.
  - o Discuss what was done well, what could be done better.

Note: Evaluations will not normally be based on isolated minor incidents (para. 3-2f)

Administrative Data (para. 3-7):

- The minimum authorized period for an NCOER is 90 rated days. (3-7c(1))

  - o Reports not requiring 90 days are: Relief for cause and Senior Rater Option and 60 Day Option (see paras. 3-32, 3-34, and 3-35). (3-7c(1))

- February is considered as having 30 days. (3-7c(1))

Duty Description (para. 3-9):

THE EVALUATOR

- Entered by rater and verified by rated NCO.

- An outline of the normal requirements of the specific duty position.

- Should show type of work, not changing tasks.

- May be updated during the rating period.

Rules for Bullet Statements (para. 3-10):

Any technique aimed at making specific words, phrases or bullets stand out from the rest may not be used including but not limited to:

- Be short, concise, to the point.

- No longer then 2 lines.

- Start with action verbs or possessive pronouns.

- Should use past tense.

- Be double-spaced.

- Preceded with a small "o."

- Each bullet should start with a small letter unless it's a proper noun.

- Authorized abbreviations may be used.

Prohibited Narrative Gimmicks (para. 3-16):

- No handwritten comments.

- No excessive use of capital letters.

- No underlining.

- No italics or other techniques.

- No exaggerated margins.

- No single spacing between comments.

- No more then one bullet per line

Note: The following comment was extracted from NCOER updates concerning bullet statements:

THE EVALUATOR

- Line up bullets: There is no regulatory guidance that says the second line of each bullet should go right under the small "o." The rule of thumb is to be consistent. If the second line starts under the "o" then all bullets should be completed in that manner (EREC TIBITS, March 2000).

Army Physical Fitness Test Entry (para. 3-11)

- Enter "PASS" or "FAIL" and the year and month of the APFT results. (3-11a)

- If no PT test is taken due to profile the entry will be "PROFILE" and the year and month the profile was awarded. (3-11a)

- The APFT entry will reflect the NCO's status on the date of the most recent record APFT administered by the unit within the 12-month period. (3-11a)

- Numerical scores will be used to justify "needs improvement" ratings based solely on APFT. (3-11a)

- Rater will explain "FAIL" or "PROFILE" entries. Comments will address reason for failure and note progress toward meeting physical fitness standards. Concerning profiles the comments will describe the rated NCO's ability to perform assigned duties. **If the rated NCO has appeared before a MOS medical retention board and been determined fit for duty and deployable, rating officials may not state that the profile hinders duty performance. (3-11b(1))**

- If the APFT has not been taken within 12 months of the THRU date and the soldier is not on a profile, the APFT data entry will be left blank. (3-11b(2))

  - The rater will explain the absence of an APFT entry. (3-11b(2))

THE EVALUATOR

o **Personnel who meet Army minimum standard for APFT but fail to meet unit standards will not be given a rating of "needs improvement" for physical fitness and military bearing if such rating is based solely on the failure to meet unit standards. (3-11c)**

Height and Weight Entry (para. 3-12):

- Absence of HT/WT data must be explained (3-12b(1))

- The statement within body fat standards is no longer required. (3-12a)

- If a NO entry is entered a comment will be entered indicating the reason for non compliance (3-12b(2))

- The progress or lack of progress in a weight control program will be indicated (3-12b(2))

- For pregnant NCOs the entire entry is left blank. Enter the comment "Exempt from weight control standards of AR 600-9." (3-12b(3))

Overall Performance and Potential (para. 3-13):

- **Among the Best**: NCOs who have demonstrated a very good, solid performance and strong recommendation for promotion and service in positions of greater responsibility. (3-13a(1))

- **Fully Capable**: Good performance and strong recommendation for promotion should sufficient allocations be available. (3-13a(2))

- **Marginal**: Poor performance and should not be promoted at this time.

THE EVALUATOR

- **Ratings of 1, 2, or 3: (3-13c)**

  - 1 and 2: represents *cream of the crop*, solid performance and is a recommendation for immediate promotion. A "2" represents a *very good* solid performer and is a strong recommendation for promotion.

  - 3: also represents ***good performance*** and should sufficient allocations be available, a promotion is recommended.

- **Rating of Fair "4":** NCOs who ***may require additional training*** and observation and ***should not be promoted*** at this time.

- **Rating of Poor "5": NCOs who are** *weak or deficient* **and in the opinion of the senior rater,** *need significant improvement* **or training in one or more areas.** *Do not promote.* **Consider for DA- imposed bar to reenlistment under the QMP program.**

Senior Rater Narrative Rules (para. 3-13d):

- Bullet comments are mandatory.

- Marginal ratings given in part Va and fair or poor ratings in part Vc must be addressed by the senior rater.

- Bullet comments should focus on potential but may address performance.

Stand Alone Reports (para. 3-15):

- Each report must stand alone. (3-15a)

- Reports will not refer to prior or subsequent reports. (3-15a)

THE EVALUATOR

- Reports will not remark on performance or incidents occurring before or after the rating period. Determination will be based on the date the actual incident or performance occurred, not on date of discovery, confession, finding of guilt, or completion of an investigation. (3-15a)

- Exceptions to this are granted for Relief for Cause reports (see 3-15b(1)) and APFT. (3-15b)

Unproven Derogatory Information (para. 3-17):

- No reference will be made to unverified derogatory information. References may only be made to derogatory information verified through thorough investigations conducted to completion and adjudicated, and upon which final action was taken before submitting the NCOER. If the NCO is absolved, comments about the incident will not be included. (3-17a-b)

- No reference will be made to an incomplete investigation (formal or informal). (3-17a)

- Any verified derogatory information (that is already proven factual by a preponderance of the evidence) may be entered on an NCOER. (3-17d)

- This is true whether the NCO is under investigation, flagged, or awaiting trial. (3-17d)

- The fact that an NCO is under investigation or trial may not be mentioned in an NCOER until the trial is completed. (3-17d)

- This does not preclude the rating chain's use of verified derogatory information. (3-17d)

THE EVALUATOR

Prohibited Comments (para. 3-18):

- Remarks or comments referring to race, color, religion, gender, and national origin are prohibited. (3-18a)

- No mention of any punitive or administrative actions (taken or planned) may be made. This does not prevent mentioning the underlying misconduct that served as the basis for the action. (3-18b)

Comments about Marital Status (para. 3-19):

Comments favorable or unfavorable will not be based solely on an NCO's marital status. In addition, comments cannot be made about the employment, educational, or volunteer activities of an NCO's spouse. (3-19a-b)

    Comments not allowed:

- "MSG Doe and his wife make a fine team." (3-19a)

- "As a bachelor SFC Doe can quickly react to his unit's contingency missions." (3-19a)

- "Mr. Doe's participation in post activities is limited by his civilian employment." (3-19b)

- "Mrs. Doe has made a significant contribution to soldier morale by her caring sponsorship of the hospital volunteer staff." (3-19b)

    Comments that are permitted under limited circumstances include incidents involving actual and demonstrable effects on the rated NCO's performance or conduct. Comments must be focused on the rated NCO's actions, not those of the spouse. (3-19c)

- o "SSG Doe's continued outstanding, selfless service, despite her husband's severe illness..." (3-19c)

- o "SGM Doe's intemperate public confrontations with his wife were detrimental to his status as a noncommissioned officer." (3-19c)

Alcohol and Drug Abuse Program (para. 3-22):

- An NCO who voluntarily enters the drug and alcohol program that has not been detected by the chain of command should not be penalized by mentioning the program on his NCOER.

- However, in cases where alcohol or drug abuse has resulted in substandard performance or disciplinary problems, subsequent voluntary enrollment does not preclude rating officials recording the substandard performance on the NCOER.

- Once an NCO has been identified in an NCOER as having an alcohol or drug abuse problem based on information obtained independently of the ADAPCP:

  - o Voluntary entry in the program or successful rehabilitation should be mentioned as a factor to the rated NCO's credit. (3-22a)

  - o The rating chain should note status of rehabilitation progress or outcome in the NCOER or in later reports. (3-22b)

- Rating official cannot use information derived from ADAPCP records in their evaluations.

THE EVALUATOR

Performance as an Equal Opportunity NCO (para. 3-26): NCOs serving as either a principle or appointed duty will not be given an unfavorable evaluation solely because of the enthusiasm and zeal with which they implement the Army's Equal Opportunity Program, or in retaliation for criticism of command policies and practices related to that program.

Types of Reports:

Annual Reports (para. 3-29): To be submitted 12 months after the most recent of the following events:

- Ending month of last report.
- Effective date of promotion to sergeant.
- Reversion to NCO status after serving as a commissioned officer or warrant officer for 12 months or more.
- Reentry on active duty in the rank of sergeant or above after a break in enlisted service of 12 months or more.

Note: Annual reports will not be signed prior to the first day of the month following the ending month of the report. Also, if the rater dies, is relieved, reduced, absent without leave, declared missing, or incapacitated, the senior rater will complete both the rater and senior rater portions of the NCOER.

Change of Rater Reports (para. 3-30): will be submitted whenever the designated rater is changed as long as the minimum rater qualifications are met. Change of Rater reports may be necessary when:

- Rater or rated NCO is reassigned.
- Rater or rated NCO departs on extended TDY or SD.
- Rater or rated NCO is released from active duty.

THE EVALUATOR

- Rated NCO is reduced to CPL/SPC or below. (Reduction to another NCO rank does not require a report unless the rater changes.)

- Rater dies, is relieved, reduced, AWOL, declared missing, or becomes incapacitated (see details in para. 3-29e).

- Mandatory when rated NCO is separated form active duty.

Note: Change of rater will not be signed before the date the change occurs. In the event of PCS, ETS, or retirement the report may be signed up to 10 days prior to the date of departure

Temporary Duty, Special Assignment, or Compassionate Reassignment Reports (para. 3-31): will be generated under the following conditions, provided rater qualifications are met prior to departure (para. 2-4):

- To attend resident training at a service school that is 90 days or more in length. (3-31a(1))

- To attend civilian academic or training institute for 90 days or more. (3-31a(2))

- To perform duties not related to his primary functions in the parent unit under a different immediate supervisor for 90 days or more. In cases where it cannot be determined if the TDY or SD will last for 90 days, a report will be submitted. A report is not authorized if the NCO will still be responsible to, or receiving instruction from, rating officials in the parent unit. (3-31a(3))

- An NCO who is TDY or SD, who is not responsible to rating officials in his parent unit, will be rated by the TDY or SD supervisor according to Table 3-5. The TDY or SD supervisor will ensure that the rating scheme is published. (3-31b)

- An NCO attached to an organization pending compassionate reassignment remains responsible to his parent unit and will not receive an evaluation report from the attached organization. Memorandum input from the supervising officials of the attached organization is mandatory (see Table 3-5, note 1). (3-31d)

Relief for Cause Reports (para. 3-32):

- Relief for Cause reports are required when an NCO is relieved for cause regardless of the rating period involved. (3-32a)

- A Relief for Cause report occurs when the NCO's personal or professional characteristics, conduct, behavior, or performance of duty warrants removal in the best interest of the Army. (3-32a)

- If relief is contemplated on the basis of an informal AR 15-6 investigation, the referral procedures contained in that regulation must be complied with prior to acting on, initiating or directing the relief. This does not preclude temporary suspension from assigned duties. (3-32b)

- The rating official directing the relief will clearly explain the reason for relief in part IV if he is the rater and in part Ve if he is the senior rater. (3-32c(1))

- If the relief is directed by an official other than the rater or senior rater, the official directing the relief will describe the reason for relief in an enclosure (not to exceed one page in length). (3-32c(2))

- Regardless of who orders the relief, the rater will enter the following statement in part IVf of the NCOER: "The rated NCO has been notified of the reason for relief". (3-32c(3))

- The minimum rating period for a relief for cause is 30 days. (3-32c(4))

THE EVALUATOR

  o The purpose of this time frame is to allow the rated NCO a sufficient period to react to performance counseling. (3-32c(4))

  o Authority to waive the 30-day period in clear-cut cases of misconduct is granted to general courts-martial jurisdiction over the relieved NCO. The waiver of the approval will be in memorandum format. See para. 3-24. (3-32c(4))

- Date of the relief determines the THRU date. (3-32c(5))

- Relief for Cause reports may be signed at any time. (3-32c(5))

- In cases where the rated NCO has been suspended from duties this time will be counted as non rated time (3-32d)

Complete the Record Reports (para. 3-33): At the option of the rater, a Complete the Record may be submitted on a NCO who is to be considered by a centralized promotion board for promotion, school, or CMS selection as long as the following conditions are met:

- Rated NCO must be in the zone of consideration (primary/secondary) for promotion or selection.

- Rated NCO must have been under the same rater for at least 90 days as of the ending month established in the message announcing the zones of consideration.

- Rated NCO must not have received a previous report for the current duty position.

Notes: (1) Since this report is an option, absence of the report will not be used to request a standby reconsideration. **(2)** Reports will not be signed prior to the first day of the month following the ending month.

THE EVALUATOR

Senior Rater Option (para. 3-34):

- When a change in senior rater occurs, the senior rater may direct that a report be made on any NCO for whom he is the senior rater. This applies only in the following conditions:

    o The senior rater has served in that position for at least 60 days. (3-34a(1))

    o The rater meets the minimum requirements. (3-34a(2))

    o The rated NCO has not received a report in the proceeding 90 rated days. (3-34a(3))

Sixty-Day Option (para. 3-35):

- When a condition listed in paras 3-29 through 3-31 occurs, and there are fewer than 90 days but more than 59 rated days in the rating period, a report may be submitted at the option of the rater. The following conditions must be met:

- NCO must be serving in an overseas designated short tour for 14 months or less. (3-35a)

- The senior rater must meet minimum requirements and must approve or disapprove submission of the report. If disapproved, the senior rater will state the basis for the disapproval and return the report to the rater. (3-35b)

Evaluations (paras. 3-2f and g):

- Should cover failures as well as achievements.
- Will not normally be based on an isolated minor incident.

THE EVALUATOR

Report Codes by Type (para. 3-37, Table 3-1):

- **Code 1**: First report (does not apply to Active Army)

- **Code 2**: Annual

- **Code 3**: Change of Rater

- **Code 4**: Complete the Record

- **Code 5**: Relief for Cause

- **Code 6**: Release from AT/ADT/ADSW/TTAD (see Chapter 5 of AR 623-205)

- **Code 7**: 60-day Rater option

- **Code 8**: Senior Rater option

Summary

It's important to know the regulation or at least be able to locate information contained in the regulation. While AR 623-205 is the primary source for NCOER, it is important to understand that other regulations may contain useful information related to the NCOER, counseling, relief for cause reports, or other similar topics. Review the publications at the beginning of this chapter; these publications should provide an adequate foundation concerning issues and situations surrounding NCOERs.

Note: Prior to initiating a relief for cause NCOER, I would suggest contacting your JAG, PSB, and higher headquarters concerning the action. In certain cases the 30-day time frame can be waived by a general officer. (Check with your local S-1/PSB for information concerning who is given this authority in your area). However, in most cases the 30-day requirement will not be waived. Be sure to follow any local guidelines and policies concerning relief actions. Some major commands even have published supplements concerning relief for cause reports.

Note: Appeals will be discussed in Chapter 4 of this book and Relief for Cause Reports are discussed in Chapter 5.

CHAPTER TWO

PREPARING THE NCOER FROM START TO FINISH

THE EVALUATOR

Preparing the NCOER from Start to Finish

Publications for Review:

- **AR 623-205**   Noncommissioned Officer Evaluation Reporting System
- **AR 600-20**   Army Command Policy
- **AR 600-9**   Army Weight Control Program
- **AR 600-37**   Letters of Reprimand
- **AR 350-41**   Training in Units
- **AR 27-10**   Military Justice
- **FM 22-100**   Leadership
- **FM 22-101**   Counseling
- **DA FORM 2166-8-1** NCOER Counseling Checklist
- **DA FORM 2166-8** NCOER Form

Local Items for Possible Review:

- **Local Policy Letters**
- **MACOM Directives**
- **Supplements to ARs**
- **NCOER Updates**

Possible Web Sites for Review:

- **PERSCOM ONLINE: www.perscom.army.mil**

- **Army Counseling Web site: www.counseling.army.mil**

- **Enlisted Records and Evaluation Center: www.erec.army.mil**

THE EVALUATOR

Prior to the Initial Counseling

As a rater, you should be well prepared prior to the initial counseling session. By being prepared, a rater sends a clear message that he cares about the soldier and wants to provide him with every opportunity to succeed. Preparation does much to establish credibility with the soldier. A counseling that is poorly constructed can destroy credibility and trust in a relationship that has not even begun. Do your best to be prepared. Ask yourself this question, "How would I feel if someone counseled me in an unprepared manner or gave me unclear guidance?"

The following is a list of items that the rater should consider prior to the initial counseling:

- **Review the publications and forms listed above.**

- **Develop an outline for your written counseling:**

    o   What do I expect from every soldier? (loyalty, trust, integrity, etc.)

    o   What will I not tolerate?

    o   What is the soldier's duty title?

    o   What is the rating chain?

    o   What are the duties and responsibilities associated with the duty title?

    o   What are the soldier's additional duties?

    o   What are the special areas of emphasis the soldier should concentrate on?

    o   What are the standards I expect the soldier to maintain?

THE EVALUATOR

o What do I want the soldier to accomplish within 30, 60, 90 days from the initial counseling?

o Does the duty title, additional duties, special areas of emphasis require additional training? If yes, does the soldier have the training or has the soldier been scheduled to attend the training?

o Questions for the soldier:

- Does the soldier have any issues that he needs to bring to your attention? (These may include family, personal, financial, medical or spiritual issues.)

- What are the soldier's expectations from the job?

- What are the soldier's near- and long-term goals?

- Does the soldier wish to pursue education?

- Does the soldier plan on requesting off-duty employment?

- **Develop the counseling.**

o Once you have examined these questions and any others you may have added to the list, put your thoughts to paper. Develop an in-depth initial counseling covering all the aspects of the job, training, expectations, rating chain, and standards. In the counseling explain what constitutes an excellent rating. This counseling should be made on a DA Form 4856 with continuation pages if required. In addition it is very important to put the highlights of the counseling on the DA FORM 2166-8-1. On the –1 also place the statement, "See attached 4856 dated_____ for details of counseling". Use the attachment because you cannot cover all the areas required for a good counseling or be detailed enough in the space provided on the 2166-8-1.

- Obtain a copy of the rating scheme.

- Develop a working copy of the NCOER: look at other NCOERs from individuals who may have held the duty position before to get ideas for the duty description. Fill out the rating chain on the working copy, additional duties, and special areas of emphasis.

- Develop a packet for the soldier. Place in this packet items the soldier may need and should be given. Examples may include copies of the rating scheme, the working NCOER, and the completed 2166-8-1 (copy made (after counseling); examples of excellence bullets; copy of initial counseling signed by both parties; unit recall roster; and home phone numbers of key personnel.

- Prepare a detailed counseling of what you expect from the soldier. My initial counseling usually outlines duties, responsibilities, additional duties, areas of special emphasis, appearance, physical fitness, formations, discipline, communications, equal opportunity/sexual harassment, education, and comments from the soldier concerning his expectations of the my leadership. (Samples of counseling may be found in "The Mentor.") Once you have properly prepared the counseling outline and statement, you are ready to notify the soldier.

- **Notify the soldier concerning the following information:**

  o Location of the counseling (ensure this is an environment free of interruptions).

  o Time (make sure it does not conflict with other unit activities).

  o The purpose of the counseling.

THE EVALUATOR

- **Conduct the counseling session**:

  o Show the soldier your draft duty description (on the working copy of the NCOER); ask the soldier to review the duty description and determine if there are any additional items or modifications that you may have overlooked.

  o Suggest that the soldier maintain a folder or notebook of accomplishments or achievements. This should be brought to each counseling session; it helps to ensure a fair report. It also gives the soldier the opportunity to provide input into the NCOER. The file may contain awards, certificates of achievement, letters of appreciation, grade slips from college courses, 1059 (academic evaluation reports), weapons and APFT information on the soldier and squad, section, platoon, or any other information that may assist the rater in preparing an NCOER.

- Find out if the soldier has any immediate concerns or needs.

- Determine short- and long-term goals.

- Are courses available to assist the soldier in accomplishing their assigned duties

- Review the rating chain, working copy of the NCOER, duty phone and home phone numbers of immediate supervisors.

- Encourage your soldiers to be innovative and bring new ideas to your attention

- Schedule your next counseling session.

- Sign and initial counseling forms (both DA FORM 2166-8-1 and DA FORM 4856).

- Provide a copy of documents to the soldier.

THE EVALUATOR

As future counselings are conducted the rater should utilize daily observations and information provided by the soldier with supporting documentation to fill in the working of copy of the NCOER. By utilizing this method the soldier always understands exactly where he stands concerning their rating. In addition, if a soldier is performing in a substandard manner it should be recorded during the counseling session and specifically addressed. In cases of substandard performance I would encourage the use of monthly counseling. This counseling should contain the substandard performance, recommendations for improvement, corrective training, and the consequences for failing to achieve the standard. There should be no surprises on a soldier's NCOER.

THE EVALUATOR

Sample DA Form 2166-8-1 (NOCER Checklist)

COUNSELING

1. Go over each part of the duty description with rated NCO. Discuss any changes, especially to the area of special emphasis.

2. Tell rated NCO how he / she is doing. Use your success standards as a guide for the discussion (the examples on pages 3 and 4 may help). First, for each value/responsibility, talk about what has happened in response to any discussion you had during the last counseling session (remember, observed action, demonstrated behavior and results). Second, talk about what was done well. Third, talk about how to do better. The goal is to get all NCOs to be successful and meet standards.

3. When possible, give examples of excellence that could apply. This gives the rated NCO something to strive for, REMEMBER, EXCELLENCE IS SPECIAL, ONLY A FEW ACHIEVE IT! Excellence includes results and often involves subordinates.

4. Ask rated NCO for ideas, examples and opinions on what has been done so far and what can be done better. (This step can be done first or last).

BEFORE THE NCO DEPARTS THE COUNSELING SESSION

1. Record counseling date on this form.
2. Write any additional key points that came up during the counseling session on this form. .
3. Show key points to rated NCO and get his/her initials.
4. Save NCO-ER with this checklist for next counseling session. (Notes should make record NCO-ER preparation easy at the end of the rating period.

COUNSELING RECORD/KEY POINTS MADE

INITIAL Discussed duties and responsibilities, areas of emphasis, additional duties, duty description, explained expectations/standards, provided a copy of rating scheme, emergency contact numbers, examples of bullets that constitute excellence in each area, reviewed working copy of NCOER, 4856 (initial counseling) and provided a copy of all documentation to soldier. Directed soldier to maintain an accomplishment folder containing all positive achievements during this rating period. See 4856 dated 1 Jan 02 for complete details of counseling

| | DATE | 01 Jan 02 | RATED NCO'S INITIALS |

LATER Overall performance has been satisfactory, soldier needs to concentrate on preparing the squad for the ARTEP in May 02. Provided training guidelines for ARTEP, expressed concern that soldier is placing too much emphasis on off duty employment and college studies (may be interfering with job performance), informed soldier if the trend continues I will recommend to the Chain of Command that off duty employment and college privileges be suspended. In addition I will consider placing a needs improvement bullet comment on his NCOER, See 4856 dated 1 Mar 02 for details of counseling.

| | DATE | 1 Mar 02 | RATED NCO'S INITIALS |

LATER Conducted special counseling with soldier concerning off duty employment and college studies. It is apparent that these items are interfering with his ability to perform his duties as a squad leader. I have recommended that the 1SG/CDR suspend/revoke off duty employment. Informed soldier that a needs improvement bullet comment will be placed on a working copy of the NCOER, if performance does not improve it will be reflected on the NCOER. See 4856 dated 7 May 02.

| | DATE | 7 May02 | RATED NCO'S INITIALS |

LATER Job performance has improved greatly, squad performed well during the ARTEP, will remove needs improvement bullet from working copy of the NCOER, continue to maintain the standard, prepare the squad for upcoming BN Lane Training, prepare SPC Joe for the promotion board 5 Sep 02, soldier provided input from the accomplishment folder concerning squad PT avg score of 280, all soldiers qualified expert, annotated working copy of NCOER. See 4856 date 1 Aug 02

| | DATE | 1 Aug 02 | RATED NCO'S INITIALS |

DUTY DESCRIPTION (PART III of NCO-ER)

The duty description is essential to performance counseling and evaluation. It is used during the first counseling session to tell rated NCO what the duties are and what needs to be emphasized. It may change somewhat during the rating period. It is used at the end of the rating period to record what was important about the duties.

The five elements of the duty description:

1 & 2. Principal Duty Title and Duty MOS Code. Enter principal duty title and DMOS that most accurately reflects actual duties performed.

3. Daily Duties and Scope. This portion should address the most important routine duties and responsibilities. Ideally, this should include number of people supervised, equipment, facilities, and dollars involved and any other routine duties and responsibilities critical to mission accomplishment.

4. Area of Special Emphasis. This portion is most likely to change somewhat during the rating period. For the first counseling session, it includes those items that require top priority effort at least for the first part of the upcoming rating period. At the end of the rating period, it should include the most important items that applied at any time during the rating period (examples are preparation for deployment, combined arms drills training for FTX, preparation for NTC rotation, revision of battalion maintenance SOP, training for tank table qualification, ITEP and company AMTP readiness, related tasks cross-training, reserve components annual training support (AT) and SIDPERS acceptance rate).

5. Appointed Duties. This portion should include those duties that are appointed and are not normally associated with the duty description.

THE EVALUATOR

Filling Out the Front of the DA Form 2166-8 (NCOER)

NCO EVALUATION REPORT			
For use of this form, see AR 623-205; the proponent agency is ODCSPER		SEE PRIVACY ACT STATEMENT IN AR 623-205, APPENDIX C.	

PART I - ADMINISTRATIVE DATA

a. NAME (Last, First, Middle Initial) 3-7d(1)	b. SSN 3-7d(1)	c. RANK 3-7d(2)	d. DATE OF RANK 3-7d(3)	e. PMOSC 3-7d(4)

f. UNIT, ORG., STATION, ZIP CODE OR APO, MAJOR COMMAND 3-7d(5)	g. REASON FOR SUBMISSION 3-7d(6)

h. PERIOD COVERED		i. RATED MONTHS	j. NON-RATED CODES	k. NO. OF ENCL	l. RATED NCO COPY (Check one and Date)		m. PSC Initials	n. CMD CODE	o. PSB CODE
FROM	THRU				1. Given to NCO	Date			
YYYY MM 3-7d(7)	YYYY MM 3-7d(7)	3-7d(8)	3-7d(9)	3-7d(10)	2. Forwarded to NCO	3-7d(11)	3-7d(12)	3-7d(13)	3-7d(14)

PART II - AUTHENTICATION

a. NAME OF RATER (Last, First, Middle Initial) 3-8c(1)	SSN	SIGNATURE	
RANK, PMOSC/BRANCH, ORGANIZATION, DUTY ASSIGNMENT 3-8c(5)			DATE
b. NAME OF SENIOR RATER (Last, First, Middle Initial) 3-8c(1)	SSN	SIGNATURE	
RANK, PMOSC/BRANCH, ORGANIZATION, DUTY ASSIGNMENT 3-8c(5)			DATE
c. RATED NCO: I understand my signature does not constitute agreement or disagreement with the evaluations of the rater and senior rater. I further understand my signature verifies that the administrative data in Part I, the rating officials in Part II, the duty description to include the counseling dates in Part III, and the APFT and height/weight entries in Part IVc are correct. I have seen the report completed through Part V, except Parts IId and IIe. I am aware of the appeals process of AR 623-205.	SIGNATURE 3-8c(2)		DATE
d. NAME OF REVIEWER (Last, First, Middle Initial) 3-8c(1)	SSN	SIGNATURE	
RANK, PMOSC/BRANCH, ORGANIZATION, DUTY ASSIGNMENT 3-8c(5)			DATE
e. ☐ CONCUR WITH RATER AND SENIOR RATER EVALUATIONS ☐ NONCONCUR WITH RATER AND/OR SENIOR RATER EVAL (See attached comments)			

PART III - DUTY DESCRIPTION (Rater)

a. PRINCIPAL DUTY TITLE 3-9b(1)	b. DUTY MOSC 3-9b(2)

c. DAILY DUTIES AND SCOPE (To include, as appropriate, people, equipment, facilities and dollars)

The rater completes and verifies with the rated NCO; address the most important daily/routine duties and responsibilities.

3-9b(3)

d. AREAS OF SPECIAL EMPHASIS   Enter AKO email addresses for the Rating Chain.

3-9b(4)

e. APPOINTED DUTIES

3-9b(5)

f. COUNSELING DATES 3-9b(6)	INITIAL	LATER	LATER	LATER

PART IV - ARMY VALUES/ATTRIBUTES/SKILLS/ACTIONS (Rater)

a. ARMY VALUES. Check either "YES" or "NO". Comments are mandatory for "No" entries; optional for "Yes" entries.

		YES	NO
	1. LOYALTY: Bears true faith and allegiance to the U. S. Constitution, the Army, the unit, and other soldiers.	X	
Loyalty	2. DUTY: Fulfills their obligations.	X	
Duty	3. RESPECT/EO/EEO: Treats people as they should be treated.	X	
Respect	4. SELFLESS-SERVICE: Puts the welfare of the nation, the Army, and subordinates before their own.	X	
Selfless-Service	5. HONOR: Lives up to all the Army values.	X	
	6. INTEGRITY: Does what is right - legally and morally.	X	
	7. PERSONAL COURAGE: Faces fear, danger, or adversity (physical and moral).	X	

V A L U E S

Honor
Integrity
Personal Courage

Bullet comments

o bullet comments are mandatory to address "NO" ratings and are optional for "YES" ratings

3-10c

DA FORM 2166-8, OCT 2001   REPLACES DA FORM 2166-7, SEP 87, WHICH IS OBSOLETE   USAPA V1.01

THE EVALUATOR

Filling Out the Back of the DA Form 2166-8 (NCOER)

RATED NCO'S NAME (Last, First, Middle Initial)	SSN	THRU DATE
+ 3-7d(1) Enter soldiers' AKO email address.	3-7d(1)	3-7d(7) +

PART IV (Rater) - VALUES/NCO RESPONSIBILITIES   *Specific Bullet examples of "EXCELLENCE" or "NEEDS IMPROVEMENT" are mandatory.*
Specific Bullet examples of "SUCCESS" are optional.

b. COMPETENCE
- o Duty proficiency; MOS competency
- o Technical & tactical; knowledge, skills, and abilities
- o Sound judgment
- o Seeking self-improvement; always learning
- o Accomplishing tasks to the fullest capacity; committed to excellence

EXCELLENCE   SUCCESS   NEEDS IMPROVEMENT
(Exceeds std)   (Meets std)   (Some)   (Much)

o bullet comments are mandatory to address 'excellence' or 'needs improvement' ratings

o bullet comments are optional but 'recommended' for 'success' ratings

3-10f

c. PHYSICAL FITNESS & MILITARY BEARING
- o Mental and physical toughness
- o Endurance and stamina to go the distance
- o Displaying confidence and enthusiasm; looks like a soldier

EXCELLENCE   SUCCESS   NEEDS IMPROVEMENT
(Exceeds std)   (Meets std)   (Some)   (Much)

APFT   HEIGHT/WEIGHT

o bullet comments are mandatory to address APFT failure and/or 'NO' entry for height/weight

o bullet comment is mandatory to address 'profile' entry

o no bullet comment if body fat standards are met   3-10f

d. LEADERSHIP
- o Mission first
- o Genuine concern for soldiers
- o Instilling the spirit to achieve and win
- o Setting the example; Be, Know, Do

EXCELLENCE   SUCCESS   NEEDS IMPROVEMENT
(Exceeds std)   (Meets std)   (Some)   (Much)

o mandatory and optional comments are the same as Part IVb above

3-10f

e. TRAINING
- o Individual and team
- o Mission focused; performance oriented
- o Teaching soldiers how; common tasks, duty-related skills
- o Sharing knowledge and experience to fight, survive and win

EXCELLENCE   SUCCESS   NEEDS IMPROVEMENT
(Exceeds std)   (Meets std)   (Some)   (Much)

o mandatory and optional comments are the same as Part IVb above

3-10f

f. RESPONSIBILITY & ACCOUNTABILITY
- o Care and maintenance of equipment/facilities
- o Soldier and equipment safety
- o Conservation of supplies and funds
- o Encouraging soldiers to learn and grow
- o Responsible for good, bad, right & wrong

EXCELLENCE   SUCCESS   NEEDS IMPROVEMENT
(Exceeds std)   (Meets std)   (Some)   (Much)

o mandatory and optional comments are the same as Part IVb above

3-10f

PART V - OVERALL PERFORMANCE AND POTENTIAL

a. RATER. Overall potential for promotion and/or service in positions of greater responsibility.

3-13a

AMONG THE BEST   FULLY CAPABLE   MARGINAL

b. RATER. List 3 positions in which the rated NCO could best serve the Army at his/her current or next higher grade.

3-13b

e. SENIOR RATER BULLET COMMENTS

o bullet comments are mandatory

o comments 'must' address potential, but may also address performance and/or evaluation rendered by rater

o ratings of 'marginal', 'fair', or 'poor' in Part V must be addressed

o if senior rater lacks qualification to render evaluation, enter "senior rater does not meet minimum qualifications"

3-13d

c. SENIOR RATER. Overall performance

3-13c

1   2   3   4   5
Successful   Fair   Poor

d. SENIOR RATER. Overall potential for promotion and/or service in positions of greater responsibility.

3-13c

1   2   3   4   5
Superior   Fair   Poor

DA FORM 2166-8, OCT 2001   USAPA V1.01

THE EVALUATOR

DA Form 2166-8 by the Numbers

PARA	Description	Explanation
3-7d(1)	Name	Self-Explanatory (**Name will be capitalized**) on the backside of the form in the name block include the **AKO account of the soldier**
3-7d(1)	SSN	Self-Explanatory
3-7d(2)	Rank	3 Letter abbreviation (Not Pay grade)
3-7d(3)	Date of Rank	6 digit date of rank yymmdd
3-7d(4)	PMOSC	Enter up to 9 digits of Primary MOS code examples include: 19E30, 75H5MA3, 18Z5PW9LA. **IAW EREC Tidbits update winter spring 2000.** An example of the 9 digit MOSC configuration is: 18B/5/O/00/OO. **Notice digits 6 & 7 are O, not zeros.**
3-7d(5)	Unit Organization	Enter data in the order listed on the form
3-7d(6)	Reason for Submission	02 Annual, 03 Change of Rater, 04 Complete the Record, 05 Relief for Cause, 06 Release from AT/ADT/ADSW/TTAD, 07 60 day rater option, 08 Senior Rater option
3-7d(7)	Period Covered	Enter 4 digit year and 2 digit month example 2001 12
3-7d(8)	Rated Months	Total number of months (from-thru) minus any non-rated time (use table 3-2) enter this amount in block I
3-7d(9)	Non-rated Codes	See Table 3-3 Para 2-3 **A**=AWOL/Desertion, **B**=break in service of 12 months or less, **C**=Confinement, **D**=Temporary disability retirement list, **I**=In transit between duty stations (including leave and TDY), **M**=Missing in Action, **P**=Patient (including con. Leave), **Q**=Lack of rater qualification, **R**=New Recruiter Program, **S**=Student at military service or civilian school, **W**=Prisoner of War, **Z**=None of the Above
3-7d(10)	Authorized Enclosures	Enter the number of authorized enclosures
3-7d(11)	Rated NCO Copy	Enter handwritten or typed X and 6 digit date yymmdd
3-7d(12)	PSC Initials	Enter handwritten initials
3-7d(13)	CMD Code	Enter NCO's MACOM code from AR 680-29
3-7d(14)	PSC Code	Enter 4 position alphanumeric PSB code
3-8c(1)	Names of Rating Chain	Self-Explanatory
3-8c(5)	Rank, PMOS, etc.	Contains 3 letter Rank abbrev unless a MSG is occupying a SGM position
3-8c(4)	Concur/Nonconcur	Place a handwritten or typed X in appropriate box

DA Form 2166-8 by the Numbers (Continued)

PARA	Description	Explanation
3-9b(1)	Duty Title	Enter principle duty title that most accurately reflects actual duties performed
3-9b(2)	Duty MOSC	At least 5 characters but no more then 9
3-9a(3)	Daily duties/scope	Address the most important routine duties and responsibilities. Ideally # of people supervised, equipment, facilities, $ involved.
3-9b(4)	Areas of Emphasis	Can change during the rating period, should include most important items that apply at any time during the rating period. **(Note: The last line of this block will be reserved for email addresses of the rating chain. Use AKO accounts when available if using AKO accounts the address will stop at the @ symbol. Example: Rater: Top.nco@.S/R: Top.officer@drum.army.mil Rev: Gijoe.Dawg. It is preferred that you use AKO accounts. This information was extracted from: Milper message number 02-114**
3-9b(5)	Appointed duties	Appointed duties not normally associated with the duty description
3-9b(6)	Counseling dates	Enter 6 digit date obtained from DA Form 2166-8-1. The absence of counseling will not be used as the sole basis for an appeal
3-10c	Values (Part IV a)	Place an X in the appropriate block, statements should be short, concise, and to the point. **Comments are mandatory for No ratings and must be specific.**
3-10f	Part IV b-f	**Excellence:** specific, measurable examples. **Success:** meets all standards. **Needs Improvement:** missed meeting some standard, specific bullet can be used only once. **Bullets are mandatory for Needs Improvement ratings.**
3-12	Part IV c HT/WT	Enter HT in inches, WT in pounds. And Yes or No to indicate that the individual meets HT/WT standards: example: 72/180 YES. No entries must be specifically explained.
3-11	Part IV c APFT	Enter Pass or Fail to indicate if the individual passed or failed the APFT or enter PROFILE and the year and month the profile was awarded. APFT can be used up to 12 months. Examples PASS 8601/FAIL 8602, PROFILE 8603. **Comments are mandatory for fail or profile entries.**
3-13a	Rater Overall Potential	Place an X in the appropriate block: Among the Best, Fully Capable, Marginal
3-13b	3 Positions	List 3 positions the NCO is capable of serving in at the current or next higher grade.
3-13c	Senior Rater	Place an X in the appropriate boxes concerning performance and potential.

THE EVALUATOR

NCOER Counseling Checklist

Action	Remarks
Has reception and integration counseling been conducted on this soldier previously? If not include it during your counseling session.	
Review AR 623-205.	
Read the NCO Counseling Checklist DA Form 2166-8-1.	
Review previous duties descriptions of individuals who have held the position.	
Develop an outline for your written counseling.	

Include in the counseling:
• Your expectations.
• The rating chain.
• Duties and responsibilities.
• Appointed duties.
• Areas of emphasis.
• Additional duties.
• Define the standards.
• Define short/long term goals.
• Does the soldier plan on continuing his education?
• Is the soldier seeking off duty employment?
• Prepare a list of examples that demonstrate what the soldier must achieve to receive excellence.
• Have the soldier maintain an accomplishment folder.
• Allow the soldier to provide input:
  o Does the soldier have any questions?
  o What are the soldier's expectations of the job?
  o What does the soldier expect from you as a leader?	

Write your counseling and review it.	
When writing your counseling use both the DA Form 2166-8-1 and a DA Form 4856.	

THE EVALUATOR

<u>NCOER Counseling Checklist (Continued)</u>

Action	Remarks
Prepare a working copy of the NCOER.	
Make copies of all documents: 1 for soldier, 1 for rater, 1 for file	
Notify the soldier of the time, place and purpose of counseling.	
Advise the soldier to be prepared to discuss his duties/responsibilities and be prepared to provide input and insight into what he believes is important.	
Ensure the area is free from distractions.	
Schedule adequate time for the counseling and ensure that it does not interfere with unit requirements.	
Be prepared when the soldier arrives for the counseling session.	
Prior to the soldier's arrival review the counseling packet once more.	
Free your mind of distractions.	
It is very important that you not only listen to what the soldier says but that you observe his body language. Up to 75% of communication is non-verbal.	
If you detect nonverbal communication explore your observations and seek clarification.	
Avoid personal bias, judgment, and losing control of your emotions.	
As you close the counseling session ask the soldier to summarize the counseling session. Have the soldier state what he expects from you and what you expect from him.	
Have the soldier initial the 2166-8-1.	
Have the soldier sign the 4856.	
Provide the soldier copies of: o The working copy of the NCOER o The rating scheme o The 2166-8-1 o The 4856 o Sample of Excellence bullets o Emergency contact numbers	
Establish a follow-up date.	

CHAPTER 3
BULLET COMMENTS

THE EVALUATOR

Value Bullets

"No" statements must be as specific as possible. Detail all bullets to fit the specifics of the conduct or incident.

1. Loyalty: Bears true faith and allegiance to the U. S. Constitution, the Army, your unit, and other soldiers.

YES Statements

- Extremely dedicated and absolutely loyal.

- Always professional and loyal to his superiors and the command.

- Extremely loyal.

- Absolutely loyal to the chain of command.

- Displays absolute loyalty to superiors.

- Unquestionable integrity and loyalty to all.

- Displays the highest standards of loyalty and integrity.

- Exhibits the highest standards of loyalty and personal courage.

- Is disciplined and obedient to the spirit and letter of all lawful orders.

- Is committed to the ideas and principles of the nation.

- Loyal and faithful in all matters.

- Builds and inspires loyalty in subordinates, peers, and superiors alike.

- Is loyal to the chain of command.

- Loyalty is beyond reproach.

- A faithful and loyal leader who cares about the mission and his soldiers.

- Encourages and inspires pride and loyalty in his subordinates.

THE EVALUATOR

NO Statements

- Consistently displays a disloyal attitude among subordinates.
- Breached his trust and loyalty among members of the chain of command.
- Makes negative comments to subordinates concerning command decisions and members of the chain of command.
- Incites a seditious attitude among subordinates.
- Held meetings with subordinates in an attempt to incite relief of a superior.
- Is not consistently loyal to the ideas of the nation; manipulates subordinates for self gain.
- Displays inconsistent loyalty and cannot be depended upon.
- Has misrepresented the facts for personal gain.
- Displays unwillingness to conform or maintain the Army ethic.
- His lack of loyalty endangers the ability of the unit to perform its mission.
- Does not understand the importance of loyalty and commitment.
- Fails to understand the impact of disloyal behavior on the unit and mission.
- Has made disloyal statements concerning the commander in chief and our nation.
- Made disloyal and threatening statements of violence toward members of the chain of command.

2. Duty: Fulfills obligations.

YES Statements

- Dedicated to the mission.
- Dependable and committed to mission accomplishment.
- Provides quality and timely professional development, advice, and guidance.
- One of the most dedicated NCOs I've ever encountered in my military career.
- Hard worker, dependable, and totally dedicated to the mission and the Army.
- Totally dedicated to the support of the academy's mission.

THE EVALUATOR

NO Statements

- Encourages subordinates to advance by cheating.

- Places personal interests above professional obligations.

- Fails to adequately supervise, mentor, and guide assigned personnel.

- Fails to assist soldiers in solving problems.

- Does not counsel subordinates.

- Does not take corrective action.

- Makes decisions based on personal feelings and bias.

- Applies himself only if the task will benefit his interest.

- Is not dependable, must have constant supervision to achieve minimum standards.

3. Respect: Treat people as they should be treated.

YES Statements

- Fully supports EO/EEO programs

- Consistently treated soldiers with dignity and respect.

- Strongly enforced fair treatment of all soldiers.

- Did not hesitate to address unfair perceptions, statements, or actions.

- Is empathic when dealing with soldiers.

- Always fair when dealing with soldiers.

- Treats others as he would want to be treated.

- His soldiers respect and appreciate his caring attitude; always treats them with dignity and respect.

- Does not tolerate abusive or demeaning behavior.

- Respected by all members of this command.

- Approaches all situations with an open mind.

- Inspires fair treatment, dignity, and respect among his soldiers.

THE EVALUATOR

- Has successfully mentored previously uncooperative soldiers to be respectful of others.
- Utilizes individual differences to strengthen the overall team.
- Creates opportunities for individuals to learn about each other.
- Instills respect of other cultures, customs, and religions in his soldiers.

NO Statements

- Does not support EO/EEO; uses demeaning and abusive language toward other races and ethnic backgrounds.
- Fails to cooperate with individuals who have different points of view.
- Aggressive when dealing with others.
- Does not treat people with dignity and respect.
- Speaks to subordinates in an abusive tone.
- Is demeaning in both voice and actions.
- Has made statements that are not respectful of other cultures, customs, and religions.
- His lack of respect for others is prejudicial to the good order and discipline of this command.
- Is closed-minded; refuses to be empathic when dealing with subordinates.
- Used racial slurs when verbally counseling a soldier.
- Fails to correct prejudicial actions, statements, or perceptions.
- Encourages prejudicial actions, statements, and perceptions among his soldiers.
- Encourages the use of stereotypes among his subordinates.

4. Selfless service: Put the welfare of the nation, the Army, and your subordinates before your own.

YES Statements

- Truly cares for soldiers and their families.

THE EVALUATOR

- Totally committed to the success of the Army.
- Stellar example of selfless service to the Army and the nation.
- Sincerely cares for the soldiers' welfare and always displays a positive attitude when considering their desires in professional development decisions.
- Inspires and motivates soldiers to meet the same high standards that he maintains.
- Committed to the unit's soldiers and mission.
- Dedicated to the mission.
- Selfless devotion to mission and subordinates.
- Is selflessly committed to mission accomplishment.
- Totally dedicated to the Army's mission.
- Strong team player.
- A true team player.
- Places dedication and commitment to the goals and mission of the Army and nation above personal welfare.
- Willingly sacrifices personal interests to benefit the ideas of the nation and the Army.

NO Statements

- Places personal gain above his commitment to his soldiers, the Army, and the nation.
- Evaluates a situation for personal gain before making a commitment.
- Not a team player; seeks personal gain over mission success.
- His competitive spirit interferes with mission accomplishment and developing a cohesive team.
- His selfish attitude destroys teamwork and promotes individualism and mission failure.
- Consistently displays an uncaring attitude.
- Places self-interest above all other factors.
- Fails to contribute to the overall effort unless he is given special recognition.
- Seeks personal recognition and gain above mission accomplishment.

THE EVALUATOR

5. Honor: Lives up to all the Army values.

YES Statements

- Personal conduct is always above reproach.
- His word is his bond.
- An honorable soldier who instills the Army values in his subordinates.
- Mentors soldiers and develops honor, courage, and commitment.
- Honor is his watchword.
- Respected as an honorable soldier.
- Sets and maintains the highest standards of honor and trustworthiness.
- Can be trusted in both word and deed.

NO Statements

- Does not conduct himself in an honorable fashion.
- Does not uphold the Army value of honor; is not trustworthy.
- Cannot be trusted to make honorable decisions; seeks self-gain.
- Has placed his honor in question; is insincere.
- Displays a dishonorable and unscrupulousness attitude.

6. Integrity: Do what's right, legally, and morally.

YES Statements

- Extremely honest.
- Epitome of integrity and reliability.
- Always fair and honest.
- A no-nonsense leader; direct and to the point.
- Always honest and fair regardless of the situation.

THE EVALUATOR

- Possesses the highest standards of integrity and moral conviction.
- Integrity is beyond reproach.
- Absolutely honest and dependable.
- Possesses flawless integrity.
- Maintains the highest standards of integrity, demands the same from others.
- Unquestionable integrity and loyalty to all.
- Displays the highest standards of loyalty and integrity.
- Always stands for and does what's right.
- Is honest and truthful in word and deed.
- His word is his bond.

NO Statements

- Lacks integrity.
- Has placed his integrity in question on numerous occasions.
- Untruthful in critical situations.
- Cannot be trusted to tell the truth.
- Modifies the truth to achieve personal gain.
- Has placed other soldiers' careers in jeopardy by distorting the truth.
- Has used his position and authority to distort the truth and endanger the career of another soldier.
- Leaders are forced to second-guess his statements due to repeated violations of integrity.
- Cannot be trusted in word or deed; consistently places his integrity in question.
- Fails to tell the truth when confronted with stress or pressure.
- Endangers the lives and welfare of his subordinates by refusing to provide honest and truthful reports; tells superiors what they want to hear.

7. Personal courage: Face fear, danger, or adversity (physical and moral).

THE EVALUATOR

YES Statements

- Performs exceptionally well under pressure and without supervision.

- Not afraid to voice his opinion and stands up for what's right

- Exhibits the highest standards of loyalty and personal courage.

- Always exercises sound judgment; thrives under pressure.

- Decisive in ethical dilemmas.

- At his best under pressure.

- Always chooses the hard right over the easy wrong.

- A trusted leader and problem-solver in a crisis.

- Has the moral conviction to stand by hard decisions.

- Displays unwavering moral courage and conviction when confronted with ethical dilemmas.

- Always stands up for what's right.

- Voices his opinions and stands up for what is right.

- Does not hesitate to address unfair perceptions, statements, or actions.

- Has the courage, conviction, and ability to overcome fear.

NO Statements

- Avoids confrontations and difficult situations at all costs.

- Does not work well under pressure.

- Indecisive during difficult situations.

- Allows and condones unethical behavior.

- Does not have the intestinal fortitude to correct substandard performance.

- Refuses to correct racist or prejudicial behavior.

- Unable to deal with crisis situations or incidents that involve stress or pressure.

- Waivers in the face of adversity.

- As a 1SG stated "I quit"; could not handle the pressures of the job.

THE EVALUATOR

COMPETENCE BULLETS OF EXCELLENCE

Awards

- Achieved 100% SIDPERS timeliness for 12 consecutive months; received Army Achievement Medal.

- Achieved three honor platoon awards during rating period.

- First choice reporter on prestigious MacArthur Awards ceremony in Pentagon-Lauded by Chief of Public Affairs for 117 releases to media.

- His battalion aid station received Post Aid Station of the Quarter Award out of 28 aid stations.

- Instrumental in the company receiving the division logistics award three months in a row.

- Prepared Ft. Bragg entry and won FORSCOM-wide Unit Ministry Team Award for 1989.

- Professional competence resulted in three battalions winning the Quarterly Excellence Award for personnel.

- Provided expertise that assisted supply in winning Division Quarterly Supply Award.

- Received ACOE Customer Service Excellence Award in September 1990.

- Received Armor School's outstanding Instructor Award for demonstrated Excellence in Tactical Skills

THE EVALUATOR

- Received AUSA Award for being selected Soldier of the Quarter.

- Received Aviation Logistics School safety award for 2 year superior performance.

- Selected for outstanding Public Service Award for 1990.

- Winner of a highly competitive role model award from the Federally Employed

- Won commanding General's Best Mess Award for second quarter FY91 Women, Adelphi Chapter.

Basic skills

- A D&C expert who reestablished the brigade drill team, resulting in two of his NCOs being accepted to all Army Drill Team.

- Provided quick first aid to his crewman which saved the soldier's finger.

- Won Honor Platoon with a platoon average of 96% in all EOCT areas.

Competition

- Barracks selected as the post representative in the TRADOC Community of Excellence Competition.

- Battery named best at ground defense by the commanding general at Ft. Bliss.

- Dining facility received a 1st Place rating from the Health Promotion Council.

- Has been selected as "Top Nurse Recruiter" for first and second quarters of FY89.

THE EVALUATOR

- Had best LANCE FDC IN 1988 VII Corps "Best Section Competition.

- His newspaper rated as MACOM best in Keith L. Ware competition.

- His guidance produced a MACOM Connelly winner in Best Field Kitchen competition.

- His radio teletype team won the Brigade and III Corps Artillery Communications Competition.

- His squad area selected as best in battalion and DISCOM by CG/ADC.

- Nominated for the agency's Technician of the Year.

- Selected as Drill Sergeant of the Quarter, then went on to be the first female Drill Sergeant of the Year for the installation.

- Selected as a finalist for the White House Military Office Senior NCO of the Year.

- Selected as NCO of the Year for Ft. Benjamin Harrison.

- Won Ft. Sheridan land navigation course competition.

- Won Third Region Soldier of the Year Competition

Deployment

- Constant belief in 24/7 combat readiness resulted in squad's ability to deploy in less than 12 hours in support of a Marne Lightning Exercise.

THE EVALUATOR

- Hand-picked to perform as Battalion S-3, Battalion Operations NCO, and HHD 1SG for a deployed battalion.

- His platoon received outstanding results on ARTEP and during the American, British, Canadian, and Australian Exercise.

- In the absence of an officer, commanded the detachment on two separate missions at JRTC.

- Instrumental in the brigade's success while serving as rail load NCOIC during NTC 97-09 loading 500 pieces of equipment.

- Orchestrated the preparation of the battalion's deployment to Africa in support of Operation Distant Rescue.

- Received the CG's coin of excellence for distinguishing himself during a corps exercise.

Development

- Authored and completed the Norddeutschland Community Physical Security Plan.

- Counseled 28 students through rating period; 100% graduated, 5 honored.

- Collected, rewrote, and published unit SOPs in 1 month; all done after the normal duty day.

- Designed, contracted, and installed computer systems for 3 APODs and ASG Headquarters.

THE EVALUATOR

- Designed and implemented a PAC training team, 10% improvement in soldier actions timeliness.

- Developed battalion multimodel deployment binder, winning praise from group commander and setting the group standard.

- Developed a billet SOP that was adopted as the TAACOM standard and was given to the USAREUR commander as a model for all billets.

- Developed a worldwide database, enabling him to quickly contact 1SGs and commanders in the field by phone and e-mail.

- Developed and implemented a database tracking system for over 5,000 maps and blueprints that greatly improved the battalion S-2.

- Developed and implemented an intensive hands-on evaluation for MOS certification.

- Developed and implemented a unit tactical checklist that received praise from several evaluators during the unit external evaluation.

- Developed and produced the first military musical ensemble performance at the Eastman School of Music.

- Developed a system to monitor SSSC account which will save thousands of dollars.

- Developed two theater-level order of battle databases from scratch.

- Developed, wrote, and published SOP for use by watch NCOs of echelon-above-corps intelligence unit.

THE EVALUATOR

- During off-duty time rewrote or created all SOPs for the platoon, which earned commendable ratings.

- Personally developed dental tracking program that raised dental readiness to 96%.

- Planned and conducted two land navigation course which resulted in 100% "GO" for entire platoon.

- Planned for, established, and implemented standards used at all Desert Storm Forward Operating Bases.

- Proposed, developed, and documented the revision of the CMF 76 SGM authorizations.

- Researched, designed and executed highly realistic cavalry scout combat training program at the NTC.

- Rewrote, edited, collected, and published a 600-page TACSOP in two months, including many after-duty hours

- Rewrote Infantry NBC ANCOC POI that was certified by Sergeant Major Academy.

- Wrote Directed Energy Warfare training pamphlet displaying excellent staff skills.

- Wrote the SOP on radio training enabled cross-training of TV producers and 100% cross-marketing of TV news to radio product.

THE EVALUATOR

Dollars & percentages

- Achieved 100% SIDPERS timeliness for 12 consecutive months; received Army Achievement Medal.

- Coordinated and developed a $70K upgrade plan to support a major dining facility renovation project.

- Coordinated the movement of 184,000 pounds of equipment worth over $2.5 million, maintaining 100% accountability.

- Ensured 100% of military leave and pay transactions were processed, exceeding DOD timeliness standards.

- Guidance and training programs improved SW scores by 9.5% to a 92 average with no failures.

- Instrumental in achieving 99% of quarters occupied, exceeding the DA and TRADOC goal.

- Instrumental in his platoon receiving a 98% first-time pass rate in weapons qualification.

- Instrumental in reducing Qualified Not Enlisted rate from 8% to all-time low of 1.8%.

- Maintained 100% SIDPERS rate even under arduous Operation Desert Storm conditions.

- Maintained a 100% SIDPERS accuracy rate for all transactions for 12 months.

THE EVALUATOR

- Maintained an 80% solve rate on investigative actions which is USACIDC's goal.

- Maintained material denial rate to 0% from an average of 6,000 material release orders per month.

- Maintained the late NCO-ER rate at 0% for eight consecutive months.

- Maintained SIDPERS rating of 100% for past 12 months.

- Played a key role in earning over $5,000 for the battalion recycle program.

- Planned and executed two fund-raisers, earning over $1,400 for soldiers' care projects.

- Prioritized travel of all Army replacements during operation Just Cause, meeting 100% of DA requirements.

- Processed 30,000 memoranda and 125,000 data entries with 99% accuracy, maintaining 48-hour backlog.

- Processed over 1,000 VSI/SSB applications with a crew of 3 soldiers with 0% late.

- Processed over 200 evaluations for all four military services; error free and achieved an exceptional 98% on time rate.

- Reduced postage expenditures by 32% despite a rate increase.

- Set up and controlled a 300-line PLL valued at $62,000 during Operation Desert Storm.

THE EVALUATOR

- Super attention to detail resulted in 100% accuracy of processing 880 new trainees.

- Took command of failing station and led it from 50% mission accomplishment to over 110%.

Education

- Completed associates degree with a GPA of 4.0.

- Completed bachelors degree with honors during this rating period.

- Completed 196 hours of correspondence work.

- Completed eight hours towards master's degree while spending over 170 days in different field exercises and unit rotations.

- Completed nine credit hours towards a masters degree during this rating period; only needs one additional class to obtain degree.

- Distinguished Honor Graduate of the Traffic Management Accident Investigation Course.

- Distinguished honor graduate of the WRAMC Paraprofessional Intensive Care Course Nov. 1999.

- Graduated the Battle Staff NCO course with a 90% academic average.

- Selected as Honor Graduate at the Foreign Language Training Center, Europe.

THE EVALUATOR

- Trained all six of his mechanics to earn mechanics badges while completing over 60 credit hours of military correspondence courses in his time off.

Inspections

- Achieved an outstanding rating on 3 out of 4 command inspections, best in the battalion.

- Always exceeded standards on unit inspections by having the best NBC room in the DISCOM.

- Brought an inherited unsatisfactory supply section to a commendable rating within a month for the Bn CIP.

- Catalyst during the FY91 Command Inspection, 17 areas were rated as outstanding.

- Complimented personally by the TRADOC IG for having a superior training program.

- Orderly room received commendable ratings in seven out of nine rated areas during battalion command inspection.

- Passed latest two division level inspections after coming right out of AIT and stepping into the supply sergeant's position.

- Received a commendable rating in publications management during Brigade Organizational Inspection.

- Was responsible for 16 pieces of engineer equipment which received commendable ratings during the AGI.

THE EVALUATOR

Maintenance

- Battalion command inspectors rated his equipment and shop as best in the battalion.

- His battalion has exceeded DA Standards on AH-64 readiness the past 12 months, 8 in combat.

- Maintenance section received a distinguished rating for security operations at NTC rotation 90/1.

- Received brigade commander's coin for outstanding maintenance of seven tanks during a brigade command inspection.

- Reduced calibration turnaround time from 6.3 days to 1.7 days.

- Reduced delinquency rating for his team from 6.7 percent to .17 percent

- Reduced the shop backlog from a high of 176 jobs to a low of 58 jobs within a three-month period.

- Trained all six of his mechanics to earn mechanics badges while completing over 60 credit hours of military correspondence courses in his time off.

Recognition

- Battalion color guard recognized as outstanding by the FORSCOM command sergeant major.

- Coined by the group CSM and group commander for outstanding performance of duty; praised as one of the best leaders in the group.

THE EVALUATOR

- Commended by numerous officers for his exceptional training of the national military academy of the former Soviet Republic of Moldova.

- During division warfighter, nine of his soldiers earned division commander coins and five earned division CSM coins for their superior technical support.

- Earned FORSCOM commendation for combat photo-journalism coverage.

- His ammunition squad was identified as the best in the history of AH-64A helicopter fielding.

- His reports received DIA commendations for contributing to the POW-MIA National Data Base.

- Only instructor to achieve the rating of master instructor within the NCO Academy.

- Picked as subject matter expert over 11 other NCOs to train Kuwaiti soldiers on the set-up and operation of the FSSP.

- Qualified for a position on the U.S. Army Parachute Team.

- Ranks 5th of 85 linguists on the FORSCOM competency test.

- Received a rating of Best Supply Operations during first quarter FY92.

- Received brigade commander's coin for outstanding maintenance of seven tanks during a brigade command inspection.

- Received five outstanding classroom evaluations during this report period.

THE EVALUATOR

- Received group commander's coin for outstanding performance of duty.

- Received the Medical Order of Military Merit from The Surgeon General for sustained superior performance.

- Selected as Instructor of the Cycle over 8 other instructors.

- Selected as Post NCO Instructor of the Year.

- Trained all six of his mechanics to earn mechanics badges while completing over 60 credit hours of military correspondence courses in his time off.

- Was chosen out of all CMF 67 and 68 NCOs in the Army to be the IFLS demonstrator for a worldwide conference.

Retention

- His competence enabled him to rank 3rd of 20 recruiters in mission accomplishment.

- Instrumental in the 3rd Brigade exceeding the recruitment mission by 14 percent.

- Major factor behind reenlistment program being best in size category for 7th Sig Command.

- Manages a brigade retention program which is an authorized master sergeant position.

- One of only two recruiters in company to be named "Best of the Best" in nationwide production contest.

THE EVALUATOR

- Selected as Guidance Counselor of the Year for FY 90.

- Surpassed the brigade's retention objectives by 175%.

- Won 3rd COSCOM Top Career Counselor Award for 2nd Qtr FY 89 Commander's Trophy.

- Won MACOM retention excellence award for 25th ID.

Weapons

- Briefed and demonstrated the M-1 Tank to foreign dignitaries on 2 separate occasions.

- Only NCO in the battalion to have a perfect score at Gunnery.

- Prepared six tank companies for an intense qualification gunnery with 95% pass rate.

- Scored a perfect score of 1000 points on Tank Table VIII as Tank Commander.

Works above grade or selected over others

- Selected by the commanding general to serve as the brigade command sergeant major over other senior CSMs.

- Selected over 29 other NCOs to serve as the squadron aviation life support officer in addition to his regular duties.

- Selected over SFCs in the unit to fill the first sergeant's position.

THE EVALUATOR

- Selected to assume duties of 1SG over senior NCOs.

- Selected to serve as the J3 by the JTF commander to train an ARNG staff on all aspects of TOC operations.

- Served in a captain's position, performance equal to other commissioned team chiefs.

- Served in a SGM position as a MSG while his unit deployed to Kuwait for 11 months, returning with no incidents and high morale.

- Serves as the point of contact concerning regulated medical waste for a two-state region; a position normally held by a seasoned officer.

- Took an inherited unsatisfactory section to commendable rating at NTC.

- Was selected to be installation 1SG over 19 other NCOs senior to her.

Miscellaneous

- Acted as Commander of Troops for an outstanding NCO-led review adjacent to the White House.

- Advised a multi-agency foreign material exploitation team resulting in national intel community accolades.

- Coordinated an active community relief effort through MPS (Military Postal System) to support the homeless.

- Completed the TRADOC-level Connelly evaluation of 12 installations ahead of schedule and at minimum cost.

THE EVALUATOR

- Coordinated and executed ahead of schedule the set-up of a local area network for 240 computers during the battalion move.

- Displayed technical mastery of his instrument as solo bugler during wreath-laying ceremony for the Defense Minister of Greece.

- Expertise resulted in his selection to train the Royal Saudi Air Defense Force during Desert Storm.

- Navigated 26 miles over open ocean by CRRC to selected beach landing site in storm conditions.

- Outstanding supply management supervision resulting in a drop in the average time to ship orders from 10 days down to 5.8 days.

- Reduced waiting period for Computerized Topography exams from 2 months to 1 day.

- Responsible for closing PSP 3J, shipping 45,000 tons in 1,200 containers and 1,365 trailers.

- Selected by scuba team to train 1st Group pre-scuba course.

- Simultaneously ran both internal battalion operations and customer support operations in a deployed environment.

- Successfully relocated brigade's mailrooms from Nuremberg to Bamberg, without loss of any mail service or accountability of mail.

- Unit operated flawlessly during his absence; a direct reflection of his ability to develop the tactical and technical skills of his soldiers.

THE EVALUATOR

- Was first to identify DDMT as breeding ground for Aedes Aldopictus mosquito.

COMPETENCE BULLETS OF SUCCESS

Competition

- Competed in brigade-level NCO of the Quarter Board in which he placed second of seven NCOs.

Deployment

- NCOIC of highly successful airload operation during deployment of battalion to JRTC.

- Oversaw recovery from Bosnia deployment, squadron rotations, and gunnery prep; all occurred without accident.

- Received accolades from senior observer Controller at NTC for job performance.

- TOC operations outstanding during squadron ARTEP and NTC rotation.

Development

- Arranged two musical selections and conducted stage band and 25-member chorus for chancellor of Germany performance.

- Created and standardized the battalion's personnel and equipment system, enhancing the overall battalion readiness.

- Developed and executed outstanding company-level decon training during company FTX in OCT 99.

THE EVALUATOR

- Developed and implemented a training matrix that simplified processing for both import and export of POV.

- Developed and supervised a company force protection plan for an OCONUS deployment, resulting in zero incidents or compromise.

- Developed bunker cleanup plan which resulted in 360 bunkers turned over to DEH prior to site cleanup.

- Established an NCO/soldier check ride matrix that the battalion requires all other companies to use.

Dollars & percentages

- Ensured the battalion's operational readiness rate was always 95% or higher for deployments and unit rotations.

- Improved supply reconciliation of overdue documents by 66% with expert knowledge of ammunition procedures.

Education

- Completed six semester hours during the rating period towards a bachelor's degree despite an extremely high OPTEMPO.

- Currently enrolled in college, seeking a bachelor's degree.

- Currently pursuing a master's degree with a GPA of 3.7.

- Demonstrated competence resulted in her selection as NCOIC, Preventive Dentistry Course, over five more senior NCOs.

THE EVALUATOR

- Successfully completed the Movement Control Specialist Course and was on the Commandant's List.

- Successfully completed the tough and demanding U.S. Army Special Forces Training.

- Raised GT score from 93 to 114.

- Ran outstanding Jump Master Qualification Course.

Inspections

- Coordinated EOD and Chemical Response teams to an on-site INF treaty inspection.

Maintenance

- Established a C & E maintenance support team for deployment to Bosnia.

- Implemented an effective way to manage PMCS for six wheeled vehicles, five trailers, and four generators.

Recognition

- Coined by numerous commanders/CSMs for providing exceptional support.

- Commended by commanding general for establishment and enforcement of security procedures at a remote collection site.

- Commended by the group commander for setting the standard in conducting airborne operations.

THE EVALUATOR

- Commended by Kenyan Minister of Defense for his outstanding medical instruction to over 150 Kenyan soldiers.

- Hand-picked as presidential driver during president's visit.

- Received a commendation for outstanding performance and dedication during a battalion gunnery exercise.

Weapons

- Compiled a detailed, step-by-step, range density SOP that dramatically increased range planning and execution.

- His experience and knowledge on the M2A2 provided valued information that helped form the training plan.

- Qualified expert on the M240B machine gun and 9mm pistol.

- Received a commendation for outstanding performance and dedication during a battalion gunnery exercise.

Works above grade or selected over others

- Admirably fills in for first sergeant while maintaining a positive control of his platoon sergeant responsibilities.

- Flawlessly performed the duties of G3 operations sergeant major during two brigade command post exercise.

- Outstanding performance as interim platoon sergeant led to permanent selection.

THE EVALUATOR

- Performed duties as 1SG impeccably on four occasions.

- Selected as acting battalion SGM over four other company first sergeants.

- Selected from among his peers to sit in as the brigade CSM in his absence.

- Selected over other, more senior NCOs to assume the duties of CMF 35/55 Ordnance branch team leader.

- Served as DCSLOG SGM during periods of the SGM's absence.

Miscellaneous

- Aggressively developed all aspects of his job and was never satisfied with just getting by.

- Coordinated the total fielding plan of 461 SINGARS radios for the entire installation.

- Coordinated with civilian agencies to assist her soldier in alleviating financial distress.

- Impeccable management of drill sergeant and recruiter nominees resulted in zero rejects.

- Kept the commander and staff informed through well-delivered intelligence briefings.

- Monitored the receipt, storage, redistribution, and reporting of 45,000 lines of excess supplies.

THE EVALUATOR

- Other 1SGs seek his guidance on soldier issues; strong mentor, planned and coordinated a flawless brigade change of command.

- Planned and executed an immunization program for a reserve battalion, allowing over 200 personnel to receive all required shots.

- Selected for TDY assignment in Jordan as part of a diplomatic military mission.

- Selected as primary instructor for the BDE EO lane training.

- Spent countless hours reading and watching training films to become technically proficient.

- Transitioned supply and PAC sections with soldiers out of MOS without any major problems.

- Turned previously unproductive NCO working lunches into effective problem-solving forums.

- Turned a substandard facility into a vibrant work place through hard work and devotion to the unit.

COMPETENCE BULLETS NEEDS IMPROVEMENT

- Consistently failed to meet administrative suspenses.

- Counseled by the battalion CSM for having the most disorganized platoon in the company.

- Has difficulty delegating authority.

THE EVALUATOR

- Failed Battalion Certification nine times.

- Failed to complete the requirements for the disposition of hazardous chemicals.

- Incapable of handling tasks without direct supervision.

- Routinely failed to meet given suspenses and to complete tasks in the prescribed manner.

- Through his negligence, committed two medication errors within one eight-hour shift.

- Unable to train others due to his lack of knowledge in his occupational specialty.

THE EVALUATOR

PHYSICAL FITNESS & BEARING BULLETS OF EXCELLENCE

Individual achievement

- Awarded Div Coin from CG, 82d Airborne Div for uniform appearance during the annual General Inspection.

- Biked across Georgia; 468 miles in 6 days

- Coach and starting player for 1st place division basketball team.

- Completed a physically demanding ascent to the summit of Cotopaxi, 19,757 feet.

- Consistently scores 300 on physical fitness tests.

- Developed a PT program for the staff which improved each score by at least 20 points.

- Distinguished Honor Graduate of Master Fitness Trainer Course.

- Earned the APFT Badge.

- Selected as the Army Physical Fitness award winner for BNCOC.

- Finished first in class on 10K division run.

- Led command 4 mile runs for last year with one-half pound of screws and braces in his hip.

- Portrayed image of NCO in Spirit of America Pageant before 60,000 spectators, including President Bush.

THE EVALUATOR

- Qualified for a position on the U.S. Army Parachute Team.

- Received commendation from battalion CSM for his soldiers' appearance and performance during company BCI.

- Selected as MVP for base-level softball team.

- Selected as Post Athlete of the Year.

- Selected for and competed with the All Army Women's Basketball Team, won the second-place trophy.

- Selected Tooele Army Depot's Athlete of the Year.

- Supervised PT program; 291 platoon average.

- Through his example and leadership the company average on last two APFTs was above 270.

- Won 1992 American Drug Free Powerlifting Association Men's National Competition.

Group achievement

- As company fitness trainer raised company APFT average from 236 to 262.

- Helped his clinic win the Commander's Trophy for APFT Excellence for the fourth consecutive cycle.

- Led company to current first-place standing in Post Commander's Cup intramural sports competition.

THE EVALUATOR

- Six out of seven of her soldiers scored 290 or more on the unit APFT Team; APFT average of 294.

- Through his example and leadership the company average on last two APFTs was above 270.

- Took first place in the Commander's Cup competition; won over teams from the Army, Air Force and Marines.

- With her proactive involvement, raised her platoon's APFT average from 227 to 268.

PHYSICAL FITNESS & BEARING BULLETS OF SUCCESS

Individual achievement

- A sterling example of military bearing; assertive and straightforward.

- Achieves outstanding results when confronted with limited resources, always finds a way to accomplish very tough missions.

- Adapts exceptionally well in an ever-changing, highly stressful, combat environment.

- Always presents an outstanding demeanor and military appearance.

- As DOL SGM, motivates his soldiers through self-pride to increase the unit standards of 250 point average by 20 points on the APFT.

THE EVALUATOR

- Possesses the mental and physical toughness to accomplish even the most demanding missions over long, sometimes 20-hour days.

- Runs PT with his soldiers every day, can still beat most of them.

- Despite serious injury, worked hard to overcome physical limitations.

- Displays superior self-confidence which motivates subordinates to achieve high standards.

- Developed an outstanding unit physical fitness program; improved individuals on average of 20 points.

- Led the volleyball team to win in the 21st TAACOM championships.

- Motivated his soldiers to increase their APFT average by more than 30 points.

- Scored 272 on his APFT, despite a back injury.

- Sets the example during daily physical training and unit APFT evaluations.

- Works extremely well under pressure; knows how to handle stress.

Group achievement

- Her platoon exceeds XVIII Airborne Corps standards for the APFT, the 4 mile run and the 6 mile road march.

- Her squad completed 12-mile road march in less than 3 hours.

THE EVALUATOR

- His emphasis on battle-focus PT resulted in a unit APFT average of 250, the highest of six units within the battalion.

- The platoon/section APFT scores increased by 18% due to his tough PT program.

- Led three unit sports teams to be competitive at the community level.

- Member of the unit 10K team that won first place in the AUSA 10K run.

- Motivated his soldiers to increase their APFT average by more than 30 points.

- Motivated soldiers to form up, compete and win at company-level sports teams; the first in over three years.

PHYSICAL FITNESS BULLETS NEEDS IMPROVEMENT

APFT

- Does not set the example, frequently late to PT formation.

- Failed to implement and maintain a viable PT program for his subordinates.

- Failed sit-ups and run and is making progress to meet physical fitness standards.

- Scored 130 on APFT.

- Failed to meet APFT standards for the two-mile run and sit-ups with a total score of 148.

THE EVALUATOR

Appearance

- Does not respond to correction for uniform and personal appearance.

Weight control

- Failed to maintain consistent progress in weight control program.

- Second time on weight control program within last 12 months.

THE EVALUATOR

LEADERSHIP BULLETS OF EXCELLENCE

Awards

- Awarded Bronze Star by division commander for leadership during Desert Storm.

- Awarded the Eighth U.S. Army Distinguished Leadership Award by the CINC/USFK/CFC/EUSA.

- Awarded the FORSCOM's MG Aubrey "RED" Newman Award for leadership excellence.

- His dynamic leadership resulted in the brigade winning overall REUP awards two consecutive years.

- Inspired NCOs to excellence continuously; 86 soldiers received the CINC EUSA Distinguished Leadership Award.

- Received impact ARCOM for outstanding leadership as battle captain during Operation Joint Endeavor deployment.

- Received the Eastern Sector Best MEPS award.

- Won brigade commander's leadership award.

Basic skills

- 85% of the battalion's CMF 11 soldiers earned EIB.

- Inspired 95B IET soldiers to break Post 9mm qualifying record of 98% with 99% 1st time "GOs."

THE EVALUATOR

- Provided quick first aid to his crewman which resulted in saving the soldier's finger.

Competitions

- Assisted and motivated platoon to be selected best in the company for drill and ceremony 2 cycles in a row.

- Cadets under his charge won their division in the National Parachute Competition.

- Coached and led female weight lifting team to place first in post tournament.

- Had best LANCE FDC in 1988 VII Corps "Best Section" competition.

- His battalion aid station received Post Aid Station of the Quarter Award out of 28 aid stations.

- His leadership produced a MACOM Connelly winner in Best Field Kitchen competition.

- His platoon earned the Distinguished Marching Unit designation for excellence in drill and ceremonies.

- His radio teletype team won the Brigade and III Corps Artillery Communications Competition.

- Led company to current first-place standing in Post Commander's Cup intramural sports competition.

THE EVALUATOR

- Mentored a civilian employee selected as Civilian of the Year and another selected as first runner-up for Civilian of the Quarter.

- Mentored 4 Sergeant Morales inductees, 1 Battalion NCO of the Quarter, 3 Battalion Soldiers of the Quarter.

- Mentored two drill sergeants to be selected as Battalion Drill Sergeant of the Quarter.

- Motivated squad to be selected as a finalist for the White House Military Office Senior NCO of the Year.

- Led and coached battalion biathlon team which won division competition.

- Led committee to win TRADOC Commander's Award for Excellence for an Outdoor Training Facility.

- Produced nine consecutive Group Soldier of the Month Board winners, five during the rated period.

- Selected as Drill Sergeant of the Quarter then went on to be the first female Drill Sergeant of the Year for the installation.

- Selected as NCO of the Year for Ft. Benjamin Harrison.

- Squad was selected #1 of nine squads to represent unit in the Infantry Skills Competition.

- Won Honor Platoon with a platoon average of 96% in all EOCT areas.

THE EVALUATOR

Deployment

- Conducted two FTXS, completely NCO-led.

- Deployed battalion on FTX BRIM FROST 99 with temperatures down to –40 degrees with no cold weather injuries.

- Flawlessly executed two security missions in support of Operation Desert Fox resulting in squad receiving accolades from 3rd Inf Div commander.

- His guidance produced a TOC operated solely by NCOs for Team Spirit.

- His squad successfully assaulted and defended key facilities during operation Just Cause.

- Instrumental in the brigade's success while serving as rail load NCOIC during NTC 97-09, loading 500 pieces of equipment.

- Leads by example, led team into Iraq to recover a downed Air Force pilot during Desert Storm.

- Led downed aircraft procedures for five search and rescue missions in Honduras.

- Led his squad through an enemy-infested area on a FTX without being detected.

- Performed admirably under fire during Operation Just Cause.

- Received Battalion rating of Excellence for OPFOR leader in company field training exercise.

- Responsible for complex & safe 5-day FTX; normally field grade officer duties.

THE EVALUATOR

- Supervised and trained staff to provide seven separate medical threat briefings to over 1,500 soldiers deploying to 13 different countries.

- Led the detachment during its first deployment in 27 years; initiated redeployment of unit to Germany.

- Mentioned by name for superior leadership of the quartering party during the annual external evaluation; a true professional soldier.

- Took an inherited unsatisfactory section to commendable rating at JRTC.

- Took an inherited unsatisfactory section to commendable rating at NTC.

Development

- During off-duty time rewrote or created all SOPs for the platoon which earned commendable ratings.

Dollars & percentages

- Has turned the EOD school around by greatly increasing quota utilization and reducing attrition by 35%.

- His leadership was instrumental in the 3rd Brigade exceeding the recruitment mission by 14%.

- Recognized by the Secretary of the Army for exceeding the PERSCOM Combined Federal Campaign goal of $128,000 by 11%.

- Took command of failing station and led it from 50% mission accomplishment to over 110%.

THE EVALUATOR

Education

- Only squad leader in the platoon that had 100% soldier enrollment in college courses, with three graduating this fall.

Inspections

- Led supply to pass latest two division-level inspections after coming right out of AIT and stepping into the supply sergeant's position.

- Organized, equipped and deployed 7 inspection teams to the USSR.

- Planned for, established, and implemented inspection standards used at all Desert Storm supply activities.

Maintenance

- Her emphasis on maintenance and logistics excellence led her unit to the Army Signal Command Supply of Excellence competition.

- Led and coached the maintenance section to a first-place finish on brigade 3d maintenance inspection.

- Won the daily Barracks and Maintenance Inspections Award during his first cycle.

Recognition

- Battalion recognized by CSA as Army's best electronic warfare unit.

THE EVALUATOR

- Brought an inherited unsatisfactory supply section to a commendable rating within a month for the battalion CIP.

- Commended by 21st TAACOM CSM for improving quality of life environment for single soldiers in barracks.

- Counseled and led five inexperienced senior NCOs into being best First Sergeant Team in DIVARTY.

- Directly responsible for 7 soldiers being awarded the EFMB.

- Facilities under his supervision were awarded TRADOC's Best Classroom Facilities.

- Hand-picked to march as a member of the CINCUSAREUR Honor Guard.

- His ammunition squad was identified as the best in the history of AH-64A Helicopter Fielding

- His squad area selected as best in battalion and DISCOM by CG/ADC.

- Inducted into the Sergeant Morales Club.

- Inspired soldier in her platoon to achieve Soldier of the Year honors.

- Instrumental in the company receiving the division logistics award three months in a row.

- Led and mentored 5 inexperienced platoon sergeants to form an effective leadership team.

THE EVALUATOR

- Received five outstanding classroom evaluations during this report period.

- Risked personal injury to save M1038 during a fuel-fed fire.

- Selected as Senior NCO of the Year in the Regiment.

- Training led subordinate to be top recruiter in company 7 out of 8 months.

- Under his leadership the dining facility received a 1st Place rating from the Health Promotion Council.

Retention

- Led by example by mentoring two soldiers toward successful achievement of their gold recruiter rings.

- Led retention NCOs to reduce SIDPERS processing times from 11.7 to 4.4 days.

Weapons

- Awarded Bronze Badge of Excellence in CG's marksmanship competition.

- Coached battalion marksmanship team to post championship.

- Coached service rifle team in winning the Interservice Championships.

- His crew training prior to gunnery resulted in his crew being the only one in the battalion to have a perfect score at Gunnery.

- Motivated his entire section to qualify expert with the 60mm mortar.

THE EVALUATOR

- Inspired 95B IET soldiers to break Post 9mm qualifying record of 98% with 99% 1st time "GOs."

- Instrumental in his platoon receiving a 98% first-time pass rate in weapons qualification.

- Relentless pursuit of excellence has resulted in 100% qualification for entire squad on all assigned weapons.

Works above grade or selected over others

- Due to his leadership abilities selected over other SFCs in the unit to fill the first sergeant's position.

- In the absence of an officer, commanded the detachment on two separate missions at JRTC.

- Manages a brigade retention program, which is an authorized master sergeant position.

- Placed in the position of platoon sergeant as junior staff sergeant; her platoon was always number one in company inspections.

- Selected as assistant platoon sergeant over 12 other NCOs.

- Selected by the commanding general to serve as the brigade command sergeant major over other senior CSMs.

- Selected over 29 other NCOs to serve as the squadron aviation life support officer in addition to his regular duties.

THE EVALUATOR

- Selected over 86 SFCs to be the senior instructor of Jumpmaster Branch.

- Selected to assume duties of 1SG over senior NCOs.

- Selected to serve as the J3 by the JTF commander to train an ARNG staff on all aspects of TOC operations.

- Served in a captain's position, performance equal to other commissioned team chiefs.

- Served in a SGM position as a MSG while his unit deployed to Kuwait for 11 months, returning with no incidents and high morale.

- Was selected to be installation 1SG over 19 other NCOs senior to her.

Miscellaneous

- Completed the TRADOC-level Connelly evaluation of 12 installations ahead of schedule and at minimum cost.

- Coached the entire environmental science technician staff to achieve nationally recognized certification in food service sanitation.

- Coordinated, executed, and led ahead of schedule the set-up of a local area network for 240 computers during the battalion move.

- Fielded the CSM Course twenty months ahead of the TRADOC standard.

- Guided new 2LT through complex visual information project, got commander's approval on first try.

THE EVALUATOR

LEADERSHIP BULLETS OF SUCCESS

Competition

- Motivated 3 soldiers to compete in division NCO of the Year competition.

- Selected as Instructor of the Cycle over 8 other instructors.

- Mentored the brigade Soldier of the Quarter and the second runner-up for two quarters.

- Natural leader who motivates soldiers to excel in any mission; they respond with two Soldier of the Month winners.

Deployment

- Led recovery from Bosnia deployment, squadron rotations, and gunnery prep; all occurred without accident.

- NCOIC of highly successful airload operation during battalion's deployment to JRTC.

- Planned and executed an immunization program for a reserve battalion allowing over 200 personnel to receive all required shots.

- Platoon NCOIC during the transfer of vehicles and equipment to the 9th Engineer Battalion in Kosovo deployment.

- Provided calm leadership during extended Panama crisis and operation Just Cause.

THE EVALUATOR

- Sacrificed personal time after duty to ensure that his soldiers and their families were taken care of during numerous FTX operations.

Development

- Developed NCO Certification Program for newly assigned sergeants.

- Mentored 3 soldiers to excel at SSG selection board; they received scores over 197.

- Developed and supervised a company force protection plan for an OCONUS deployment, resulting in zero incidents or compromise.

- Led, developed and executed outstanding company-level decon training during company FTX in OCT 99.

- Planned and coordinated a flawless brigade change of command.

Dollars & percentage

- Ensured the battalion's operational readiness rate was always 95% or higher for deployments and unit rotations.

Education

- As a small group leader his students maintained an academic average of 93% without any failures.

- Coordinated afternoon college courses at PSP3J, which resulted in 32 soldiers earning 9 hours of college credit.

THE EVALUATOR

Inspections

- Led S-1 section to overall satisfactory rating on command inspection with only 3 weeks notification,

- Orderly room received commendable ratings in seven out of nine rated areas during battalion command inspection.

Maintenance

- Established a C & E maintenance support team for deployment to Bosnia.

Recognition

- A dominating influence in the development of competent, tough and aggressive small-unit leaders.

- Commended by brigade commander for leadership in the orchestration of brigade change of command ceremony.

Weapons

- Ensured subordinates' weapons, equipment, and vehicles were serviceable and mission ready.

- Led the headquarters company to excel over three other companies during the battalion weapons qualification and CTT testing.

- Mentored all team members to qualify expert on all of their assigned weapons.

THE EVALUATOR

Works above grade or selected over others

- Outstanding performance as interim platoon sergeant led to permanent selection.

- Performed duties as 1SG impeccably on four occasions.

- Selected as acting battalion SGM over four other company first sergeants.

- Selected from among his peers to sit in as the brigade CSM in his absence.

- Served as DCSLOG SGM during periods of the SGM's absence.

- Successfully functioned as acting ordnance branch sergeant major on several occasions; took complete charge.

Miscellaneous

- Coordinated with civilian agencies to assist her soldier in alleviating financial distress.

- Demonstrates ability to weigh alternatives and make sound decisions.

- Motivated postal personnel to perform diligently during an extremely busy Christmas season.

- Has personally invested much of his own time and resources to improve the dining facility for the soldiers' benefit.

- Rapidly assimilated newly assigned soldiers into most productive work force in brigade.

- Supervised 101 enlisted personnel from 9 work sites, located 5 to 50 miles from hospital.

THE EVALUATOR

- This warrior sets the example by leading from the front of the best medical platoon in the Ranger Training Brigade.

- Trained and mentored junior leaders to create strongest staff section in the division

- Transformed an inherited unmotivated and unorganized unit into an aggressively motivated team.

- Turned a substandard facility into a vibrant work place through hard work and devotion to the unit.

- Turned previously unproductive NCO working lunches into effective problem-solving forums.

LEADERSHIP BULLETS NEEDS IMPROVEMENT

- Altered unit record for personal gain.

- Allowed subordinates to ignore verbal and written directives.

- Constantly complains about time spent in the field.

- Counseled by the battalion CSM for having the most disorganized platoon in the company.

- Demonstrated little concern for the security and accountability of sensitive items during cyclic field exercises.

- Does not complete mission requirements in a timely manner.

THE EVALUATOR

- Does not respond to correction for uniform and personal appearance.

- Encouraged soldiers to grow by cheating for each other.

- Failed Battalion Certification nine times.

- Failed to comply with instructions of superiors on several occasions.

- Failed to conduct monthly written counseling of enlisted soldiers.

- Failed to develop subordinates; did not perform mandatory performance counseling for the NCOER.

- Failed to follow established procedures for securing and accounting for ammunition.

- Has difficulty in delegating authority.

- Improper purchase from subordinate adversely affected morale and discipline within the section.

- Integrity compromised upon submission of false documents.

- Lack of supervision over subordinates and failure to follow procedures resulted in the loss of $2,000 worth of equipment.

- Lacks desire to work with and train soldiers.

- Many times has failed to inspect soldiers and their equipment.

THE EVALUATOR

- Misses PT formations.

- Participates in horseplay with lower-grade enlisted soldiers.

- Perception of improper conduct adversely affected morale and discipline within the division.

- Refused to do his job as 1SG of unit and said, "I quit."

- Routinely failed to meet given suspenses and to complete tasks in the prescribed manner.

- Second time on weight control program within last 12 months.

- Set a bad example by extorting money from his soldiers.

- Soldier relieved for wrongful possession of government property.

- Was relieved for driving while intoxicated in an off-duty status.

- Unexcused absence from duty left platoon enlisted soldiers unsupervised.

THE EVALUATOR

TRAINING BULLETS OF EXCELLENCE

APFT

- Commended by DIVARTY commander for teaching martial arts class to the unit.

- Developed a PT program for the staff which improved each score by at least 20 points.

Awards

- His ability to train was directly responsible for 7 soldiers being awarded the EFMB.

- Facilities under his supervision were awarded TRADOC's Best Classroom Facilities.

- Led committee to win TRADOC Commander's Award for Excellence for an Outdoor Training Facility.

- Provided expertise that assisted supply in winning Division Quarterly Supply Award.

- Received Armor School's Outstanding Instructor Award for demonstrated Excellence in Tactical Skills.

- Trained battalion and battery reenlistment NCOs to win 1st Qtr FY91 Divarty, Reenlistment Award

THE EVALUATOR

Basic skills

- A D&C expert who reestablished the brigade drill team, resulting in two of his NCOs being accepted to all Army Drill Team.

- Achieved a 15% increase in CTT scores, through effective training and follow-up.

- Assisted and motivated platoon to be selected best in the company for drill and ceremony 2 cycles in a row.

- Commended by battalion commander as having the best enlisted training program within the battalion.

- Developed and implemented an intensive hands-on evaluation for MOS certification.

- His one-on-one training resulted in Squad's 91% SQT Score, Average.

- His outstanding Sergeant's Time Training was selected as the centerpiece for a USAREUR TODAY television series.

- His platoon earned the Distinguished Marching Unit designation for excellence in drill and ceremonies.

- Produced nine consecutive group Soldier of the Month Board winners, five during the rated period.

Competition

- Coached female weight lifting team to place first in post tournament.

THE EVALUATOR

- Had top two squads in "Top Gun" Competition out of 20 squads in company.

- Has trained Ranger Challenge Team to a history making first place finish in Brigade Ranger Shootout.

- His aggressive training program resulted in 12 soldiers excelling in the Army's Culinary Arts competition, winning 16 medals.

- Placed second in TRADOC Instructor of the Year competition.

- Received 100% GO rating in Special Forces Desert Stakes.

- Squad was selected #1 of nine squads to represent unit in the Infantry Skills Competition.

- Trained Division NCO of the Year.

- Trained Forces Command Explosive Ordnance Disposal Team of the Year.

Deployment

- Conducted two FTXS, completely NCO–led.

- His guidance produced a TOC operated solely by NCOs for Team Spirit 1989.

- Received battalion rating of Excellence for OPFOR leader in company field training exercise.

- Recognized by Honduran forces as the best instructor during JTX Cabanas 89.

Development

- Counseled 28 students through rating period; 100% graduated, 5 honored.

THE EVALUATOR

- Created training plan based on the unit METL for the battalion NCO FTX.

- Developed 11B/13B BNCOC FTX-STX that has been the "model" for all Noncommissioned Officer academies.

- Designed and implemented a PAC training team, with 10% improvement in soldier actions timeliness.

- Developed a mentoring guide for soldiers that has been made available Army-wide; excellent leadership tool.

- Developed a student training handout which saved the Army an estimated $6,500 annually.

- Developed and implemented a drivers training program which licensed 12 soldiers in the section within 30 days.

- Developed a Sergeant Morales study tape that assisted junior leaders in preparing for these demanding boards.

- Developed the IG office Mission Essential Tasks List.

- Planned and executed the first annual brigade "Battle Buddy" Military Stakes Competition.

- Researched, designed and executed highly realistic cavalry scout combat training program at the NTC.

- Supervised and trained staff to provide seven separate medical threat briefings to over 1,500 soldiers deploying to 13 different countries.

THE EVALUATOR

- Rewrote, edited, collected, and published a 600-page TACSOP in two months including many after-duty hours.

- Wrote Directed Energy Warfare training pamphlet displaying excellent staff skills.

- Wrote the SOP on radio training – enabled cross-training of TV producers and 100% cross-marketing of TV news to radio product.

Dollars & percentages

- 85% of the battalion's CMF 11 soldiers earned EIB.

- Demonstrated excellent work habits and attention to detail that contributed to a 26% rise in EIB success.

- Formulated an $118,000 budget to meet all of MTMC Europe demands for training.

- Guidance and training programs improved SW scores by 9.5% to 92 average with no failures.

- Has turned the EOD school around by greatly increasing quota utilization and reducing attrition by 35%.

- His training program for 96B has resulted in 100% qualifying rate for 2 years with averages of near 90%.

Education

- Clinical instructor for 91BN3 students with a 100% pass rate of all students who have taken the National Certification Exam.

THE EVALUATOR

- Only squad leader in the platoon that had 100% soldier enrollment in college courses with three graduating this fall.

- Was instrumental in his squad increasing their GT score averages from 102 to 116.

Inspections

- Received excellent rating from 21st TAACOM IG during deployment training assessment.

Maintenance

- Her emphasis on maintenance and logistics excellence led her unit to the Army Signal Command Supply of Excellence competition.

- Trained all six of his mechanics to earn mechanics badges while completing over 60 credit hours of military correspondence courses in his time off.

Recognition

- Commended by commandant for training New York reservist.

- Commended by numerous officers for his exceptional training of the national military academy of the former Soviet Republic of Moldova.

- Commended by USAREUR IG for NCO Certification Program established for the battalion.

THE EVALUATOR

- Complimented personally by the TRADOC IG for having a superior training program.

- Constant belief in 24/7 combat readiness resulted in squad's ability to deploy in less than 12 hours in support of a Marne Lightning Exercise.

- His battalion labeled "best ever" to go through AH-64 Unit Training at Ft. Hood.

- His squad area selected as best in battalion and DISCOM by CG/ADC.

- His training resulted in the battalion being recognized by CSA as Army's best electronic warfare unit.

- Provided primary training to battalion medics, which earned the section the Division EFMB Streamer.

- Selected by scuba team to train 1st Group pre-scuba course.

- Selected to serve as the J3 by the JTF commander to train an ARNG staff on all aspects of TOC operations.

Retention

- Training led subordinate to be top recruiter in company 7 out of 8 months.

Weapons

- Coached battalion marksmanship team to post championship.

- Coached the battalion's M60 machine gun team to an overall top placement in the CG's marksmanship competition.

THE EVALUATOR

- His squad qualified expert with M9 pistol, M16A1 rifle and MP5 sub-machine gun.

- His training methods resulted in his section being the only section in the battalion to have a perfect score at Gunnery.

- His training of the section contributed to the company's 60mm being selected as best in the battalion.

- Instrumental in his platoon receiving a 98% first-time pass rate in weapons qualification.

- Marksmanship instructions resulted in 96% of the detachment firing expert with the M16A2.

- Prepared six tank companies for an intense qualification gunnery with a 95 percent pass rate.

- Relentless pursuit of excellence has resulted in 100% qualification for entire squad on all assigned weapons.

- Scored a perfect score of 1,000 points on Tank Table VIII as tank commander.

- Trained the crew which won the 32d AADCOM best crew competition, obtaining a perfect score of 1,000 points.

Miscellaneous

- Coached the entire environmental science technician staff to achieve nationally recognized certification in food service sanitation.

THE EVALUATOR

- Mentored 5 soldiers to achieve an average of 198 points on the promotion board.

- Picked as subject matter expert over 11 other NCOs to train Kuwaiti soldier on the set-up and operation of the FSSP.

- Recognized by 21st TAACOM CG for best concurrent training during Aerial Gunnery Exercise.

- Trained several leaders utilizing the train-the-trainer concept that resulted in Reserve Component leaders conducting valuable training to standard.

TRAINING BULLETS OF SUCCESS

Basic skills

- Actively seeks out field training opportunities for his soldiers/section.

- Ensured 100% of directorate passed CTT.

- Led the headquarters company to excel over three other companies during the battalion weapons qualification and CTT testing.

Competition

- Mentored the brigade Soldier of the Quarter and the second runner-up for two quarters.

- Selected as Instructor of the Cycle over 8 other instructors.

Deployment

- Sacrificed personal time after duty to ensure that his soldiers and their families were taken care of during numerous FTX operations

THE EVALUATOR

Development

- A dominating influence in the development of competent, tough and aggressive small-unit leaders.

- Established a 76Y training plan that greatly increased the job performance of subordinates.

- Developed NCO Certification Program for newly assigned sergeants.

- Developed and executed outstanding company-level decon training during company FTX in OCT 99.

- Trained two marginal soldiers to receive air traffic control facility rating.

Education

- As a small group leader his students maintained an academic average of 93% without any failures.

- Successfully completed the Contracting Officer's Representative Course.

- Successfully completed the Movement Control Specialist Course and was on the Commandant's List.

Inspections

- Used battalion command inspections as a forum to teach soldier skills and improved NBC operations.

THE EVALUATOR

Maintenance

- Because of his training no vehicles in the company have failed a roadside inspection.

- Cross-training of track vehicle repairmen has enhanced serviceability of the fleet.

- Has had no equipment down time since his arrival in our unit.

Recognition

- Commended by Kenyan Minister of Defense for his outstanding medical instruction to over 150 Kenyan soldiers.

- Received a commendation for outstanding performance and dedication during a battalion gunnery exercise.

- Selected as primary instructor for the BDE EO lane training.

Weapons

- Mentored all team members to qualify expert on all of their assigned weapons.

Miscellaneous

- Instructed an indigenous force of 140 individuals in Spanish on various subjects.

- Managed the training of over 800 ROTC cadets in squad tactics.

- Prepared doctrinal training that will lead the NCO Corps into the next century.

THE EVALUATOR

- Relieved a critical shortage of drivers within the unit through intensive classroom training & road testing.

- Responsible for training newly assigned military and civilian personnel in the collection of over 380 blood samples daily.

- Spends considerable time and effort passing his vast experience on to others.

- Successfully completed the tough and demanding U.S. Army Special Forces Training.

- Takes advantage of unscheduled time to train his section on mission essential tasks.

- Taught doctrine to civilians who successfully fielded battlefield software and interim hardware.

- Trained and mentored junior leaders to create strongest staff section in the division.

- Trained soldiers to assume next higher position at any time.

- Tough, demanding leader; always fair.

- Turned a substandard facility into a vibrant work place through hard work and devotion to the unit.

- Volunteered off-duty time to help train JROTC students.

THE EVALUATOR

TRAINING BULLETS NEEDS IMPROVEMENT

- Lacks desire to work with and train soldiers.

- Many times has failed to inspect soldiers and their equipment prior to training events.

- Training consistently below standard; despite one-on-one assistance.

- Unable to train others due to his lack of knowledge in his occupational specialty.

THE EVALUATOR

RESPONSIBILITY BULLETS OF EXCELLENCE

Awards

- His battalion received CINCUSAREUR and V Corps Safety Excellence awards.

- His chapel received Facility Beautification Award in first quarter.

- His emphasis on motor stables and equipment maintenance resulted in winning the USAREUR Army Award for Maintenance Excellence.

- Earned the Army Motor Vehicle Driver Safety Award for accident-free operation in a demanding environment.

- Emphasis on safety resulted in 9 soldiers receiving the Army Motor Vehicle Safety Award.

- Received Aviation Logistics School safety award for 2 year superior performance.

Competition

- Barracks selected as the post representative in the TRADOC community of Excellence competition.

- Won brigade competition for best housing areas twice, best on post areas once, during rating period.

Deployment

- Deployed battalion on FTX BRIM FROST 99 with temperatures down to –40 degrees with no cold weather injuries.

THE EVALUATOR

- His emphasis on safety directly contributed to 177 accident-free days during two deployments in Germany.

- His emphasis on safety resulted in his squad logging over 5,000 accident-free miles during Operation Hot Spot and IA 99-01.

- Instrumental in the recovery, accountability, and turn-in of 37 tanks left by a previous rotation at NTC.

Dollars & percentages

- 100% inventory indicated zero discrepancies of the hospital hand receipt of $2,000,000 inventory.

- Accounted for Property Book valued at over $20 million.

- Coordinated and developed a $70K upgrade plan to support a major dining facility renovation project.

- Coordinated the movement of 184,000 pounds of equipment worth over $2.5 million maintaining 100% accountability.

- Created a TACCS paper recycling program which saves thousands of dollars annually.

- Decreased supply spending by $1 million through precision troubleshooting procedures.

- Developed a system to monitor SSSC account which will save thousands of dollars.

THE EVALUATOR

- Emphasis on ammunition accountability and forecasting has allowed 100% ammo expenditure for FY 89.

- Ensured his divisional units were manned at 100% 4 months prior to the deadline established by the Chief of Staff of the Army.

- Formulated an $118,000 budget to meet all of MTMC Europe demands for training.

- Found and corrected a flaw in recoverable exchange procedures, resulting in a savings of $8,000.

- Instrumental in achieving 99% of quarters occupied, exceeding the DA and TRADOC goal.

- Maintained accountability for $8.1 million on six different property hand receipts.

- Maintained accountability for over $8 million worth of section equipment.

- Maintained 100% accuracy for 7 major subordinate command ammunition accounts valued at over $28 million.

- Maintained 100% SIDPERS rate even under arduous Operation Desert Storm conditions.

- Maintained 56 computer systems of varying types worth $160,339 at an operational readiness rate of 99%.

- Maintained strict accountability of more than $30,000 in donated humanitarian relief medical supplies for the Kosovo area.

THE EVALUATOR

- Managed $1.7 million worth of equipment at four separate work sites on the installation.

- Processed 30,000 memoranda and 125,000 data entries with 99% accuracy, maintaining 48-hour backlog.

- Reduced delinquency rating for his team from 6.7% to .17%.

- Reduced postage expenditures by 32% despite a rate increase.

- Saved directorate $100,000 by correcting list of loaned generators.

- Saved government $10,000 by buying surplus tires and rims.

- Was the key to battalion receiving $190,000 for motor pool renovation, establishing the corps standard.

Inspections

- Battalion command inspectors rated his equipment and shop as best in the battalion.

- Her squad was always number one in the company in all unit inspections and CTA 50 layouts.

- His section received commendable comments from the Group Headquarters during the Battalion Command Inspection.

- His soldiers' barracks rooms and TA-50 layout were best in the company during recent CRI.

- Received brigade commander's coin for outstanding maintenance of seven tanks during a brigade command inspection.

- Responsible for laundry and bath section receiving a 100% rating during the recent Command Inspection.

Maintenance

- Developed a platoon maintenance training program that resulted in a 95% operational readiness rate.

- Emphasis on maintenance resulted in unit placing second in the DA-level competition for the Army Award for Maintenance Excellence.

- Her emphasis on maintenance and logistics excellence led her unit to the Army Signal Command Supply of Excellence competition.

- His emphasis on care and maintenance of facilities resulted in Mainz being selected DA Community of the Year.

- Maintenance section received a distinguished rating for security operations at NTC rotation 90/1.

Recognition

- Commended by 21st TAACOM CSM for improving quality of life environment for single soldiers in barracks.

- His battalion has exceeded DA standards on AH-64 readiness the past 12 months, 8 in combat.

THE EVALUATOR

- Played a key role in earning over $5,000 for the Battalion Recycle Program.

- Successfully relocated brigade's mailrooms from Nuremberg to Bamberg without loss of any mail service or accountability of mail.

- Was responsible for 16 pieces of engineer equipment which received commendable ratings during the AGI.

Safety

- 1 out of 3 instructors awarded Post Safety Certificate for outstanding achievement in accident prevention.

- Conducted MANPADs "live fire" exercises with zero accidents or safety infractions for past year.

- Earned battalion safety recognition for driving 50,000 accident-free miles.

- Her emphasis on safety resulted in the unit having over "364 days" of accident-free and no DUI-related incidents.

- His quick response during a vehicle incident prevented serious injury to another soldier.

- Supervised MOS related safety for five facilities, resulting in 871,000 safe takeoffs/landings.

Works above grade or selected over others

- Assumed the duties of assignment manager on short notice; corrected 24-month backlog of administrative paperwork,

THE EVALUATOR

- Responsible for complex and safe 5-day FTX; normally field grade officer duties.

Miscellaneous

- Conducted the installation support modules project and demonstration for the Army Chief of Staff.

- Manufactured X-ray darkroom at no cost to the Army to provide film processing capabilities for the hospital.

- NCOIC of a ration break-down point in Honduras which issued over 45,000 meals with no loss or spoilage.

RESPONSIBILITY BULLETS OF SUCCESS

Deployment

- Provided 100% reliable secure radio teletype communications to 193d Inf BDE during Just Cause.

- Lets mechanics learn by doing and returned from REFORGER 88 with a first-rate maintenance section.

Development

- Developed and supervised a company force protection plan for an OCONUS deployment resulting in zero incidents or compromise.

THE EVALUATOR

Dollars & percentages

- Held accountable for the maintenance of over $23,000 worth of vehicle and communication equipment.

- Improved supply reconciliation of overdue documents by 66% with expert knowledge of ammunition procedures.

- Maintained 100% accountability of $42,788 worth of tools.

Inspections

- Equipment passed DMZ post operations inspection with laudatory comments.

Maintenance

- Her squad personnel, equipment, and billets are always in a high state of readiness.

- Maintained over 3,000 items of cryptographic communications equipment.

Safety

- Acted as safety officer for numerous live fire exercises without incident.

- Performed Post Safety Certification for all fuel handlers.

- Supervised a chainsaw crew operating in disaster conditions with no safety incidents during flood recovery operations.

THE EVALUATOR

Works above grade or selected over others

- Platoon NCOIC during the transfer of vehicles and equipment to the 9th Engineer Battalion in Kosovo deployment.

Miscellaneous

- His prompt self-help repairs to the buildings have contributed to efficient utilization of resources.

- Obtained 6 telemetry units for the ward despite serious roadblocks in procurement.

RESPONSIBILITY BULLETS NEEDS IMPROVEMENT

- Becomes intolerably insubordinate when counseled in regards to corrective criticism.

- Fails to care for subordinates.

- Failed to account for components of section equipment end items, resulting in marginal readiness of equipment.

- Failed to follow established procedures for securing and accounting for ammunition.

- Improper purchase from subordinate adversely affected morale and discipline within the section.

THE EVALUATOR

- Lack of supervision over subordinates and failure to follow procedures resulted in the loss of $2,000 worth of equipment.

- Many times has failed to inspect soldiers and their equipment.

- Showed little concern for maintenance of supply vehicle.

- Used his MOS proficiency to deceive supervisors and subordinates.

THE EVALUATOR

SENIOR RATER POTENTIAL BULLET EXAMPLE

- 1SG of the best battery in the battalion, must select for SGM Academy.

- Assign as a battalion CSM or commandant of an NCO Academy.

- A must for assignment as AG sergeant major.

- A dynamic, multifunctional NCO who is sought out for his extraordinary leadership capabilities

- Absolutely outstanding NCO whose performance and abilities clearly outdistance those of his peers.

- An outstanding motivator of troops; serves the Army best in leadership positions.

- An outstanding squad leader even the most unprofessional soldiers follow; this junior NCO is ready for tougher, more challenging responsibilities.

- Assign as platoon sergeant in a mechanized infantry unit.

- Assign as first sergeant to capitalize on leadership talents.

- Best squad leader in the platoon.

- Capitalize on his leadership abilities and select for Drill Sergeant School.

- Clearly capable of serving with distinction in the most demanding and critical assignments.

- Continue to challenge this NCO with increased responsibility.

THE EVALUATOR

- Destined for CSM.

- Exemplary performer with unlimited potential; excels on all assigned duties.

- Extremely versatile and capable of functioning in any capacity.

- Excellent potential for assignment to general officer level staff.

- Epitomizes the highest standards of a well-rounded professional.

- Fully capable of handling multiple crises situations and performing at next higher rank.

- Greatest potential of all maintenance team chiefs in the battalion.

- His greatest contribution to the Army will be leading and training armor soldiers in a line tank platoon.

- His impeccable leadership skills demand tough leadership positions.

- Has the drive and motivation to be an outstanding 1SG.

- Has potential to perform well at higher organizational levels.

- Is ready to be a First Sergeant nNow.

- Keep in leadership positions; he will make a difference.

- Must promote to master sergeant on first look.

THE EVALUATOR

- One of the most loyal, competent, and motivated noncommissioned officers I have ever observed in four years as a 1SG.

- Personally selected by the division CSM to become a SGM in the NCO Academy.

- Performed with maturity and leadership skills normally found in a command sergeant major.

- Promote to SFC immediately.

- Promote immediately and make NCOIC of a MEDCEN or 1SG of a medical company.

- Promote now, best platoon sergeant in the company.

- Promote now to Master Sergeant.

- Promote now to CSM, and give him a field artillery battalion.

- Promote ahead of peers and send to ANCOC.

- Promote immediately, place in leadership positions.

- Possesses exceptional potential as a division, installation, or MACOM CSM.

- Potential for major contributions as a corps artillery or division CSM.

- Rated "best" wrecker operator in the brigade by commander.

- Should not hesitate to place this soldier in demanding and critical positions.

THE EVALUATOR

- Select for attendance at Battle Staff Course.

- Select for service in positions of greater responsibility ahead of peers.

- Select for drill sergeant duty; young soldiers need his wisdom and guidance.

- Select for sergeant first class now.

- Select for CSM in the secondary zone; send to Sergeant's Major Academy now.

- Self-starter, promote ahead of peers.

- Send to ANCOC and assign as a trainer of soldiers.

- Send to ANCOC now.

- Send to ANCOC at first opportunity and assign to positions of greater responsibility.

- Send to ANCOC as soon as possible.

- Send to school, promote, and make him a battery motor sergeant.

- Superb performer, very loyal; self-starter.

- Select for drill sergeant duty; this soldier is who our newly recruited soldiers need to guide them in the right directions.

- Superior NCO, coach, and mentor, must be promoted to SFC NOW.

- Tremendous leadership potential and knowledge that will allow any squad to succeed.

THE EVALUATOR

- Trained her NBC teams to win four consecutive quarterly battalion NBC competitions.

- Is in the top 5% of all SSGs I have worked with in my past 11 years of service.

- Top-notch NCO who leads from the front.

- The best qualified of 33 SGMs in the division to assume the duties of the directorate Sergeant Major.

- The more responsibility the better; a superb motivator of soldiers.

- This SSG is ready to excel as a platoon sergeant, promote now.

- The best of my nine First Sergeants.

- The epitome of a professional NCO warrior, a model for all others to emulate.

- This NCO is a future CSM.

- Unlimited potential; must be promoted immediately and assigned as an infantry battalion CSM.

- Unlimited potential, promote ahead of peers, send to 1SG's course and assign as a 1SG.

- Unlimited potential; tomorrow's leader; promote now.

- Unlimited potential, recommend for Sergeant Major's Academy and promote.

THE EVALUATOR

- Unlimited leadership potential; recommend attendance at BNCOC as soon as possible.

- Unlimited potential; this junior NCO is ready for senior NCO responsibility.

- Unquestionably First Sergeant material; outstanding leader of soldiers.

- Will excel in positions requiring strong administrative and leadership skills.

- Would be an invaluable asset on any battalion staff.

SENIOR RATE BULLETS RELATING TO FULLY CAPABLE OR NEEDS IMPROVEMENT

Note: Remember a rating of three (3) is successful and means promote. Do not send conflicting ratings to the board members. If you mean "do not promote" the rating should be a four (4) or five (5).

- An average performer who is fully capable of being a platoon sergeant.

- Do not promote at this time (rating of 4 or 5).

- Does not apply himself; do not promote at this time (rating of 4 or 5).

- Does not display the attitude of a leader; said "I quit."

- Does not possess the qualities to perform at the next higher grade (rating of 4 or 5).

- Has the potential of being a fully capable platoon sergeant.

THE EVALUATOR

- Has the ability to perform but chooses not to apply himself.

- Fails to take responsibility for his actions.

- Lacks maturity and displays poor judgment; retain at current grade (rating of 4 or 5).

- Send to BNCOC when slots are available.

- Will make a good platoon sergeant with more experience.

- Promote only if slots are available; needs more experience.

- Send to BNCOC if slots are available; needs the additional knowledge.

CHAPTER 4

NCOER APPEALS

THE EVALUATOR

NCOER APPEALS

Publications for Review:

- AR 623-205 Appeals Process & Commander's Inquiry
- Appeal Preparation Guide

Local Sources to Consider for Assistance

- Chain of Command
- S-1
- PSB
- JAG

Possible Web sites:

- NCOER Appeal Guide:
  http://www.erec.army.mil/ncoer/NCOER_Appeal_Guide.htm

- PERSCOM: http://www.perscom.army.mil

Introduction

Appeals should be prepared with great care and attention to detail. The success of an appeal depends largely on the effort put forth by the individual making it. Service members have three forms of redress to appeal ratings on the NCOER. These include:

- **Commander's Inquiry**: This procedure is implemented IAW AR 623-205 and attempts to solve the problem before the matter becomes a part of the soldier's official record. It must be conducted by an officer who has the rank of major or above.

- **Appeals Process:** These procedures and examples are contained in AR 623-205, Chapter 4 and Appendix F. A soldier who has entered an appeal may check on the status of his appeal by contacting EREC.

- **Army Board of Correction of Military Records**: This is the final form of redress and the procedures for this action are outlined in AR 15-185.

THE EVALUATOR

Overview of the Appeal Process (IAW AR 623-205 Chapter 6)

- A commander's inquiry is not a prerequisite for submitting an appeal. However, a favorable commander's inquiry may be used to support a formal appeal (paras. 6-2 and 6-6)

- NCOERs placed in the OMPF are presumed to be administratively correct, prepared by the proper rating officials, and represent objective judgment at the time of preparation (para. 6-6).

- The signature of the NCO verifies and authenticates information contained in parts I, II, HT/WT and APFT sections of the NCOER. Appeals based solely on administrative errors in these portions will only be accepted under the most unusual circumstances (para. 6-6h(1)).

- Appeals based solely on statements from rating officials claiming administrative oversight or typographical error will normally be returned without action (para. 6-6).

- Appeals based solely on lack of full compliance with performance counseling requirements will not normally serve as a basis to invalidate an NCOER (para. 6-6h(3)).

- Substantive appeals must be made within 5 years of the NCOER's completion date (para. 6-7).

- Appeals may be granted in whole, in part, or denied (para. 6-8c).

- **Priority of appeals (para. 6-9)** (must be identified in the letter sent to the review board):

THE EVALUATOR

- o **First priority:** Appeals pertaining to NCOs who have been:

    - Twice not selected for promotion in the primary zone and are within 6 months of discharge, ETS, or mandatory retirement.

    - Selected for QMP.

    - Selected for release from AGR.

    - Identified for referral within 6 months to an AGR continuation board.

  - o **Second Priority:** Appeals pertaining to NCOs who have not been selected for promotion in the primary zone of consideration at least once, but who do not have a mandatory release date within 6 months.

  - o **Third Priority:** Appeals not eligible for higher priority but if favorably considered might result in a material change in an NCO's records.

- Burden of Proof rests with the appealing soldier and evidence must be strong and compelling and not be just a possibility (para. 6-10).

- For claims of administrative errors evidence may include (para. 6-10c):

  - o Published rating scheme used by the organization during the entire period of the report.

  - o Assignment, travel and or temporary duty orders.

  - o Extracts from personnel data cards, morning reports.

THE EVALUATOR

- o Leave records.

- o Organization manning documents.

- o Hospital admission and disposition sheets.

- o Statements of military personnel officers or others who know the situation.

- o Results of Commander's Inquiry.

- For claims of inaccuracy or injustice of a substantive type, evidence must include (para. 6-10d):

  - o Statements from third parties.

  - o Statements from rating officials.

  - o Annual General Inspection results.

  - o Award citations.

  - o Letters of Commendation.

  - o Investigation findings.

  - o Other documents attesting to the NCO's performance during the rated period.

- Do not include information unrelated to the appeal or the periods not covered during the contested NCOER.

THE EVALUATOR

Items to Consider (for an Appeal)

- Make a list of individuals who served in positions who would have knowledge of the situation, your duties, and your performance, and who might have information that could otherwise assist you in your appeal.

- If you have lost contact with these individuals, contact your local PSB or PERSCOM online, or use the Army Locator on the Web (Army Knowledge Online Account holders) to attempt to locate them.

- Prepare letters to these individuals requesting assistance in your appeal. AR 623-205 contains an example format.

- Utilize Appendix F of AR 623-205 to construct your letters to the board and request assistance.

- Utilize the local PSB, chain of command, and JAG for assistance.

Preparing for the Appeal

- Develop a rationale: The success of the appeal depends on how it is prepared, the line of the argument, and the strength of the evidence presented. Begin by specifically identifying those entries or comments you wish to challenge (the perceived injustice or inaccuracy).

- Obtain evidence: Collect all supporting evidence to support your claim.

  o If using third-party statements, ensure that these individuals:

    ▪ Have knowledge of your (rated soldier's) duty performance during the rating period.

THE EVALUATOR

- Served in positions from which they could observe your (rated soldier's) individual's performance and interactions with rating officials

- Statements should:
  - Be specific and not generalize.
  - Be provided by knowledgeable subordinates, peers, and superiors.
  - Be written on letterhead.
  - Describe the author's duty relationship with the soldier requesting the appeal during the rating period in question.
  - Include the frequency with which the author was able to make observations of the appealing soldier's duty performance.
  - Contain the author's current address and telephone number.

- Have a disinterested third party review your appeal.

- Submit the appeal in duplicate.

THE EVALUATOR

NCOER APPEAL CHECKLIST

Required documents & Entries	CHECK WHEN COMPLETED

Cover letter
• Prepared in memorandum format on letterhead or white bond paper, utilize Appendix F of AR 623-205.
• First paragraph should include:
   o That the appeal is being submitted IAW Chapter 4
   o Name, Rank, PMOS, SSN
   o Period of the report
   o Priority of appeal (see para. 6-9)
   o Identify any pending personnel actions (DA or Local bar to reenlistment or mandatory retirement)
• Include DSN or commercial phone number.
• Include correct mailing address.
• Briefly explain the nature of your disagreement.
• State what corrective action is requested.
• List and identify all enclosures.
• Sign and date the memorandum.	

Evidence
• Administrative appeals must be proven by original or certified true copies of appropriate documents
• Substantive appeals must be supported by originals of typed statements from knowledgeable observers or rating officials during the report period
• Other documents must be original or certified true copies
• Evidence may include:
   o Published rating scheme used by the organization during the entire period of the report
   o Assignment, travel and or temporary duty orders
   o Extracts from personnel data cards, morning reports
   o Leave records
   o Organization manning documents
   o Hospital admission and disposition sheets
   o Statements of military personnel officers or others that know the situation
   o Results of Commander's Inquiry
   o Statements from 3 parties
   o Rating officials
   o Annual General Inspection results
   o Award citations
   o Letters of Commendation
   o Investigation findings
   o Other documents attesting to the NCO's performance during the rated period
• Enclose a copy of the NCOER in question	

Include certified copies of your 2-1 and 2A.	
Have your packet reviewed for accuracy & completeness by an individual you trust	
Send two copies (keep one for your records).	

FOLLOW GUIDELINES IN AR 623-205 and CHECK THE EREC WEB SITE

THE EVALUATOR

SAMPLE REQUEST FOR COMMANDER'S INQUIRY

ABTC-TC   1 August 1992

MEMORANDUM FOR Commander, 198th Training Battalion, CMR 405, APO AE 09085

SUBJECT: Request for Commander's Inquiry Concerning NCOER Evaluation Report for Troubled D. Dawg, SSN: 123-45-6789, Report Ending Month: 9208

1. I am requesting that a Commander's Inquiry be initiated under the provisions of AR 623-205. I am requesting this inquiry because I believe the evaluation report lacks fairness and objectivity, and is a direct result of my rater's personal feelings rather than my professional performance during this rating period. My rater, SFC Donald E. Dawg (Senior Instructor), while being careful not to portray a negative rating, has failed to give me credit for the specific accomplishments during this rating period. Failing to recognize specific achievements, in my opinion, significantly reduces the strength of the report and does not provide an accurate picture of my performance during this rating period.

2. My specific concerns are as follows:

    a. Part IVa. Competence: I am currently the only instructor in the Basic Noncommissioned Officer Course to achieve the rating of Senior Instructor while assigned to the academy. I believe this achievement rates an "excellence." However, my rater, in order to downgrade the accomplishment, has written the bullet in the following format: 'achieved rating of senior instructor'

    b. Part IVa. Competence: I completed my associates degree during this rating period. My rater was made aware of this fact and chose to enter the following comment: "attends college after duty hours." Instead of acknowledging the completion of my degree, the rater again minimized the accomplishment.

    c. In addition, the following accomplishment was not mentioned on the NCOER: Won Instructor of the Year Competition.

3. While these points may seem minor and technical in nature, I personally believe that this is a deliberate move, on the part of my rater, to discredit me and my contributions to the academy.

4. The Senior Instructor has made it clear on several occasions that he has a strong personal dislike for me. I therefore offer the following evidence to support my claims.

THE EVALUATOR

ABTC-TC

SUBJECT: Request for Commander's Inquiry Concerning NCOER Evaluation Report for Troubled D. Dawg, SSN: 123-45-6789, Report Ending Month: 9208

a. At no time did I receive an initial or quarterly counseling or description of duties. The rating chain was not reviewed with me nor published for my review, and I have never reviewed a working copy of my NCOER. I requested to be counseled on 4 separate occasions and even made an appointment with my rater for that purpose, which he cancelled and would not reschedule. The counseling dates listed on my NCOER are false since the counseling did not happen.

b. I have had several confrontations with my rater and I believe that these situations have influenced my evaluation. The confrontations were a result of my rater attempting to use undue influence to change Academic Evaluation Reports on students who had previously worked for him. He requested that I change ratings for these soldiers. When I refused, he stated that it would reflect on my NCOER. I refused to change the ratings because the soldiers had demonstrated serious breaches of integrity and moral standard. In addition, my rater refused to surface these violations to the chain of command.

c. After the incident listed above I requested that I be removed from the academy. I spoke with my rater and stated that I could no longer trust him because he had lied to me on several occasions, and covered up criminal activity in violation of the UCMJ, and I was unwilling to continue being subjected to his abusive language and unprofessional behavior. He then made the following statement: "Bye."

5. Since my rater had failed to follow any of the counseling procedures and was unaware of any of my achievements, I gave him a list of my accomplishments for the rating period. His reply used abusive and unprofessional language. The general meaning of his comments were as follows: "I write your NCOER, Sarge, and I told you, it will reflect."

6. I have attempted to solve this problem at the lowest level and have exhausted all means at the local level. I request your assistance in this matter IAW AR 623-205. I regret having to take this action; however, I believe this evaluation is not a true measure of my performance. I appreciate your time and consideration in this matter. I may be reached at DSN: 123-4567, COM: 234-5678

TROUBLED D. DAWG
SSG, USA

THE EVALUATOR

SUMMARY

The appeal process should not be undertaken in a light-hearted manner. It is better to address the issue before it becomes a matter of your permanent record. My advice is to approach your rater and discuss your concerns with him. If this should fail address the issue with the senior rater. If you are still not satisfied formalize your request by asking for a Commander's Inquiry.

If you are proactive the Commander's Inquiry should be completed in sufficient time to correct any injustices or inaccuracies. If the report is sent forward and your Commander's Inquiry returns with findings in your favor, then it can be used to support your formal appeal.

Normally a rater or senior rater will correct errors in accuracy when provided accurate information. However, when personalities or definition of standards are involved a disinterested party may be required to review the facts of the case. I have provided a sample of a request for a Commander's Inquiry because I believe this is the best course of action should the direct approach with your rater and senior rater fail.

As a leader you can alleviate or reduce the problem of soldiers questioning your evaluations by providing proactive counseling. Counseling allows your soldiers to learn from their mistakes and attempts to correct substandard performance. If you believe a soldier is a substandard performer counsel them, put it on a working copy of their NCOER. By following this process the soldier is not kept in the dark and you have documentation to support your rating in the event the soldier chooses to appeal. **Substandard performers do not promote themselves, they are promoted by leaders who failed to do their job correctly.**

CHAPTER 5

RELIEF FOR CAUSE REPORTS
(SUGGESTIONS)

THE EVALUATOR

Relief for Cause Reports (Suggestions)

Publications for Review:

- AR 623-205
- AR 600-20

Local Sources to Consider for Assistance:

- MACOM Supplement to AR 623-205
- Chain of command
- S-1
- PSB
- JAG
- IG

Possible Web Sites:

- Enlisted Records and Evaluation Center: http://www.erec.army.mil

- PERSCOM: http://www.perscom.army.mil

Introduction

I must make it extremely clear that the **information contained in this chapter should only be used as a guide**. Since each case must stand on its own merit it is extremely important that you **seek guidance from qualified personnel** before deciding upon a Relief for Cause Report as the primary course of action. These qualified personnel may include the agencies and regulations listed above. Entering into a Relief for Cause process without proper guidance could have devastating effects on a soldier and a command. As a relieving official keep in mind that you must be fair and objective in your evaluation of the situation.

A Relief for Cause Report is a serious matter and should not be considered unless the misconduct, willful neglect, or inefficiency of an NCO warrants such action. This action can be based on personal or professional behavior. In most cases a Relief for

THE EVALUATOR

Cause Report will not be generated unless the NCO has been given a minimum of 30 days to correct his performance. In clear cases of misconduct this authority can be waived by the first general officer in the chain of command or an officer having general courts-martial jurisdiction over the relieved NCO.

If the relief is contemplated on the basis of an AR 15-6 investigation, the referral procedures contained in AR 15-6 must be complied with prior to initiating or directing the relief.

I cannot stress enough the importance of seeking guidance from qualified professionals. These professionals know and understand the requirements of a Relief for Cause and are familiar with local policies and procedures. In addition it is very important that as a leader you deal with the case based on merit and examine all the facts. Treat the individual involved as you would want to be treated in this situation.

The information that follows was collected from a series of supplements to AR 623-205 and individual experiences.

Note: It is important that you investigate the specific procedures utilized at your installation concerning the Relief for Cause process. Do not contemplate or initiate a Relief for Cause Report unless you have spoken with professionals at your installation concerning the specifics of the case.

Definitions

In order to understand the purpose of relief, let's examine a few definitions that may be useful in determining if a Relief for Cause Report is warranted.

Inefficiency: This is demonstration by an individual which reflects an NCO's inability to perform the duties and responsibilities of his rank or MOS. It is imperative that the

commander weigh all the factors before making a decision concerning inefficiency. These factors may include such considerations as:

- Has the NCO recently been reclassified into his current MOS?

- Has the individual been misassigned outside his MOS into a field that requires extensive training?

- Is there a personality conflict between the individual and a member of the command requesting the relief?

Misconduct: This refers to wrongful or improper conduct which does not necessarily involve the commission of an offense considered punishable under the UCMJ.

Willful neglect: This is related to misconduct and involves an action or actions committed with reckless disregard of consequences.

Note: Please keep in mind that most of the following information is not regulatory in nature. This information is to be used only as a guide to provoke thought and understanding of the issue. Before directing or initiating a Relief for Cause it is imperative that you contact one of the agencies listed under Local Sources, or follow the procedures established by your local command. The procedures concerning the relief of an NCO may vary from unit to unit.

Counseling

As I have previously stated, proper and professional counseling is imperative and provides clear and direct guidance to NCOs and soldiers. If the unit enforces a solid counseling program many problems will be solved at the lowest level. Moreover, if the counseling does not rectify the problem it will provide background to members of the chain of command in determining if a Relief for Cause Report is warranted. This counseling may not necessarily be negative; in fact it is possible that the counseling may reflect that the soldier's past performance has been satisfactory or even outstanding.

The record of counseling should be used to examine the whole soldier and possible reasons that may have sparked the interest in a Relief for Cause. In cases of clear misconduct, willful neglect, or inefficiency past performance may not necessarily be a factor that is considered.

With respect to a relief. AR 623-205 states that a minimum of 30 days (rating period) be established prior to the relief of the NCO. The purpose of this restriction is to allow the rated NCO sufficient time to react to performance counseling. This requirement can be waived by a general officer in clear-cut cases of misconduct.

Here are some **suggestions** you may consider when conducting the 30-day counseling. Please keep in mind that the counseling may be done by the NCO's rater or by the unit commander. **In my opinion** the unit commander should conduct the counseling. My reasoning for this is that a Relief for Cause Report is a serious event and a commander should be involved personally if the potential of relief exists for one of his NCOs. In addition, I believe that it shows the chain of command is concerned about its soldiers and takes the matter of relief seriously.

Also, a commander is also slightly removed from the situation and should be able to make decisions concerning the case without prejudice. **Again, this is only my opinion**, but I think it is important to err on the side of fairness to the individual involved.

THE EVALUATOR

Cases of Demonstrated Inefficiency or Unacceptable Duty Performance

Suggestions for Counseling:

- Formally document all records of counseling.

- Maintain a copy of counselings.

- Give the soldier a copy of all counseling documents.

- The NCO's rater or unit commander should conduct an initial counseling. The counseling should inform the NCO of his deficiencies and offer recommendations to improve duty performance.

- If no improvement is noted after the initial counseling, the officer having the authority to relieve should advise the NCO that his performance is unacceptable and that he has 30 days to correct the deficiencies.

- The NCO should be issued a memorandum of "Intent to Relieve." This memo should:

    o Be as detailed as possible.

    o Cover all known deficiencies.

    o Offer specific suggestions on methods to correct unacceptable performance.

    o Avoid generalities on how to improve performance.

THE EVALUATOR

- The officer having authority to relieve, rating chain, and commander should be present.

- During this 30 day period, counsel the NCO once a week.

- Counseling should be done by a commander.

- All improvements and deficiencies should be addressed on the counseling statement.

- At the conclusion of the 30-day period the 4 counseling statements and all other documentation should be forwarded to the officer having the authority to relieve and should be the basis for his decision to relieve the NCO.

- If sufficient progress is being made to warrant retention the evaluation process may be continued until full satisfactory performance is achieved (up to 1 year).

- If performance has not improved the NCO should be informed both verbally and in writing of the action to be taken (**continued monitoring or relief**).

- Once the counseling and Relief for Cause process is initiated it may remain in the active mode for a period of 1 year. This means that the process can be finished any time within one year without having to repeat any previous steps. This means an NCO may be given the intent to relieve memorandum, improve performance, relapse into unacceptable performance, and immediately receive another counseling, or be relieved by the officer having authority to relieve without having to start the process again.

THE EVALUATOR

Cases of Misconduct or Willful Neglect

- If misconduct or willful neglect is not severe you may follow the procedures outlined for cases of inefficiency and unacceptable performance.

- This process does not prevent the initiation of judicial or nonjudicial action.

- If considered essential by the commander an NCO may be immediately suspended but not relieved pending an investigation.

  - If suspended from duty the individual should be informed of the basis for the action, including all allegations leading to suspension

- If the facts and documents support a relief, the NCO will be informed of the decision to relieve verbally and in writing and should be provided a copy of all documents.

- In clear-cut cases in which the severity of the act warrants, the 30-day period may be waived by a general officer in the chain of command or general officer with general courts-martial authority over the NCO.

Actions After a Relief

- If judicial or administrative actions are pending the individual should be flagged as deemed appropriate.

- When possible the NCO should be placed in a completely new rating scheme.

- The NCO should at a minimum receive a new rater.

- If the relief involves a 1SG, consider action to remove the SQI of M.

THE EVALUATOR

- Comments on the NCOER should not include punitive or administrative action taken against the NCO or any investigation that has not been completed.

- If applicable the command may make recommendations to remove an NCO from a DA selection standing list for promotion or schooling.

- If deemed appropriate the command may also consider:

  o Reclassifying the relieved NCO, citing loss of proficiency.

  o Reduction for misconduct or inefficiency may be considered IAW AR 600-200.

  o Bar to Reenlistment: AR 601-280.

  o Separation: AR 635-200.

THE EVALUATOR

ITEMS TO CONSIDER DURING RELIEF FOR CAUSE

SUGGESTION	REMARKS
For cases of Inefficiency or Unacceptable Performance:	
• Review the counseling file of the NCO.	
• Has the NCO recently been reclassified into his current MOS?	
• Has the NCO been misassigned outside his MOS into a position that requires specialized training?	
• Is there a personality conflict between the NCO and a member of the rating chain?	
• Examine all the facts surrounding the situation.	
• Contact your local IG, JAG, PSB, S-1, Chain of Command for guidance.	
• Follow local procedures.	

• Consider conducting an initial counseling (rater or commander) that includes:
  o Deficiencies.
  o Specific recommendations to improve performance.	

• If unacceptable performance continues, consider issuing the NCO a memorandum of Intent to Relieve by the commander with authority to relieve. Memo should:
  o Be as detailed as possible.
  o Cover all deficiencies.
  o Offer specific recommendations to correct performance.
  o Initiate a 30-day counseling period.	

• Commander should counsel soldier weekly.	

THE EVALUATOR

ITEMS TO CONSIDER DURING RELIEF FOR CAUSE (Continued)

SUGGESTION	REMARKS
Counseling should include: • All improvements. • All deficiencies.	
At the conclusion of the 30-day period all documents should be forwarded to the relief authority for decision.	
If progress is sufficient evaluation period may be extended (up to one year).	
Relief authority should advise NCO of actions being directed (verbally and in writing).	
Cases of Misconduct or Willful Neglect	
If not severe enough to initiate relief you may follow counseling procedures listed above.	
You may consider judicial or non-judicial action.	
NCO may be suspended from duty pending outcome of an investigation.	
In clear-cut cases a general officer may waive the 30-day period to improve performance.	
Actions After Relief	
If appropriate NCO may be flagged.	
NCO should at a minimum be placed under a new rating scheme.	
Only place appropriate comments on an NCOER.	
Commander may consider: • Reclassification. • Reduction. • Bar to reenlistment. • Separation.	

NOTE: The soldier should be provided a copy of all documentation and all counseling should be formally documented. **Do not use this list as regulatory or official guidance. Check local policy and contact the S-1, PSB, and JAG. Most Major Commands may have a supplement to AR 623-205 concerning relief actions.**

CHAPTER 6

FREQUENTLY ASKED QUESTIONS AND GUIDANCE

(Note: The information contained in this chapter was extracted from the NCOER Update Website. It represents guidance from EREC and is not based on my opinion or experience.).

THE EVALUATOR

NCO-ER
FREQUENTLY ASKED QUESTIONS

Visually Centering Bullet Comments

Q: Is there a prohibition on "visually centering" bullet comments in part IV of the NCOER? For example, I wish to place just one bullet in part IVc. Instead of writing the bullet at the top of the box just under the APFT data, I would like to skip a few spaces and center the bullet in the box. Please advise.

A: Although the regulation does not specifically 'prohibit' visually centering the bullet comment, it is preferable to start all bullet comments in the same location - at the top of the designated block. This provides consistency throughout the report. It does not matter if there is only one bullet comment in the block, placing it at the top is still the desired location.

Changes to an NCOER After Submission (Inconsistencies)

Q: I received an NCO-ER that was processed through the PSB and later returned to the unit for changes (inconsistencies). I was not notified that changes were made on the report until I went to check my records and was informed that the S-1 NCO had made changes to the NCO-ER and resubmitted it without informing me of the changes. The change that was made involved whiting out the square 'among the best' that the rater had marked originally and marking the square 'fully capable'. The original NCOER was completed on a computer and had a distinctive X mark. The altered version that was sent the second time clearly has a typewriter X (the X's do not match). Is this legal?

A: This is certainly NOT the way NCO-ER processing should be done. Personnel folks in the S-1 or at the PSB are NOT authorized to alter reports. If the rater or senior rater elects to change something in his/her portion of the report, he/she must do that on their own. Also, the rated soldier should be notified when there is such a change. You should contact the rater on the report and find out if he/she authorized a change. If so, then there is not much you can do about it because the only problem here is that the rater didn't tell you about it. However, if the rater did NOT authorize the change, then you need to get that in writing - a statement signed by the rater plus a copy of the original report that was signed before the change. That then can be used as a case against the individual that changed it as well as for you to submit an appeal. It is a rather small correction and with a statement from the rater and a copy of the original report, you may be able to get this corrected quickly. However, you need to contact the appeals folks at EREC to be certain.

Duty MOS vs. Individual's MOS

Q: I have a question about the Duty MOS - is it the MOS that the soldier holds or is it the MOS that the position is slotted in?

THE EVALUATOR

A: The duty MOS is the MOS that the individual is actually working in - not the one that he/she is slotted in on the MTOE/TDA. Sometimes the position on the books is just to have the individual slotted someplace. The duty MOS and duty description that is placed on the NCO-ER should be the one that the NCO is actually working on a daily basis, regardless of what the PMOS is or the position on the books.

Appeals Process

Q: I have an active duty SFC that received a bad NCO-ER back in 9404 while stationed in Germany. I know the appeal process according to the regulation is within 5 years and the NCO did submit an appeal back in 1995. However, the appeal was denied. QMP notification happened next and the NCO appealed that and it was approved. The NCO then tried going through the Army Board for Correction of Military Records to get the NCO-ER removed and that was denied. Is there any other recourse we can take? This is an outstanding NCO and all of the other NCO-ERs on the NCO's record are great. I am just trying to figure out how I can help this soldier make MSG. Having read the entire packet and the circumstances regarding the one bad NCO-ER, I am more than convinced that the NCO got hosed, for a lack of a better term.

A: Unfortunately, the NCO has no other recourse at this point. The appeals process contains provisions to resubmit the appeal if it was initially denied due to lack of sufficient evidence/documentation to support her claims of injustice. There is no evidence that the NCO did this, but obviously chose to go directly to the ABCMR - which is the final step in the appeals process. They are usually more lenient but once the ABCMR denies the appeal, there is no other recourse. The other issue is time. The statute of limitations has expired so they wouldn't even consider another appeal at this point anyway. I spoke to EREC about this also and they cited a recent example where another NCO submitted an appeal after the statute of limitations and it was returned without action. That NCO then submitted a congressional asking for an exception to policy but that, too, was denied because there was no sufficient justification (prolonged hospitalization or deployment that prevented timely submission). 5 years is a long time so after that point, it's almost impossible to get a successful appeal. Based on additional information in your inquiry, it appears that the NCO may have come up short in putting the appeal together and maybe that contributed to the two denials. The good part is that the QMP appeal was approved. It is possible to overcome ONE bad NCO-ER and still get promoted - particularly if it was that long ago. The NCO should address it with a letter to the board when the record is being considered for promotion. The NCO could cite what was done to correct the situation and briefly explain the circumstances that led to the bad NCO-ER. The fact that all of the reports before and after that one were good is certainly a strong point to mention in such a letter. There are no guarantees but one thing is certain, it would not hurt the NCO's chances.

Maintaining Previous NCOER's From a Different Rater

Q: As a "rule of thumb", I like to see the last NCO-ER of any soldier I rate. This ensures that I don't repeat any bullets or that I don't make any administrative errors that could conflict with his/her last NCO-ER. However, my PAC informs me that I can't maintain any old NCO-ERs on file? They cited something about "personal in nature". Am I violating any regulation by maintaining my own copy of the rated NCO's last NCO-ER?

A: You are not authorized to request or maintain a copy of an NCO's last evaluation report unless YOU were the rater. If you rated the individual, then you always have the option of keeping a copy of the report YOU rendered. However, if the individual is recently assigned to you and you want a copy of his last NCO-ER rendered by some other rating officials, that is not authorized. You repeating a bullet that someone in a completely different rating chain included on the last report is not a problem or issue. Actually, if that was to happen without you knowing it, then it just validates what the previous rater stated. As for administrative data, there are ample resources to verify that data without getting it from the last NCO-ER. As for the end date of the last report, you can always call the IVRS line at DSN 221-3732 to find out the end date of the last report on file and that serves as verification of the new report FROM date.

Senior Rater Comment Guidance

Q: Currently, many of our senior leaders in the company are in debate over the acceptability of certain Senior Rater Comments and I solicit your leadership and guidance in this matter. The situation deals with SGTs and the standard line comments "Promote now" and "Select for next higher NCOES now". It is understood that these comments are necessary for Senior NCO Promotion boards but do they really benefit the E-5 team leader, when promotion to the next higher grade is dependent on the soldier's individual initiative? I hope I clearly articulated this concern. Is there any place I can research this or can you shed some light on this subject?

A: It is 'required' that senior raters address potential on ALL NCO-ERs. The specific wording that's used is up to that rating official. Potential consists of more than just promotion. It also includes schools, future assignments, and long-term advancement potential. Yes, the immediate concern is the soldier's potential for immediate advancement but rating officials should also comment on long-term potential. For example, a hard-charging, energetic and highly motivated SGT/E5 may have the following comment on his NCO-ER in the potential area:

o demonstrates exceptional initiative and potential for rapid advancement to senior NCO level

He may not even be promotable to SSG yet, but the rating official may see the POTENTIAL in that individual. The same holds true for other NCOs. Another example:

o a top-notch NCO - clearly a future command sergeant major

THE EVALUATOR

APFT Scores

Q: I am somewhat confused with the new change regarding the use of the numerical score. It is no longer required to use the score but to say that the soldier 'received the physical fitness badge'. If the soldier continuously scores 300 and above, could we still use the score if we choose to? It wouldn't seem right to say that the soldier received the physical fitness badge every year if you are only issued the badge once. Please advise.

A: It is acceptable to use the score but it is not required.

Civilians Rating NCO's

Q: According to AR 623-205 par 3-5(2b), states that a GS-6 appointed by the Commander can rate a NCO if a military supervisor is not available when that civilian is in the best position to evaluate that NCOs performance. What the regulation does not state is what rank must that NCO be in order for the GS-6 to rate him/her. Is there a regulation that shows what the equivalence rating between GS and Enlisted/Officers? For Example: Can a GS-06 rate a SFC?

A: The answer is YES, a GS-06 CAN rate a SFC. There is no specific regulatory guidance regarding rank limitations for civilians rating NCOs. However, as a general rule, a GS-06 would rate an E5 or E6; normally it would be at least a GS-07 rating SFC. Normally you don't see GS-06 rating SFC unless the GS-06 is specifically assigned to a supervisory position and that SFC is one of the NCOs in that section. Since a SFC is a SENIOR NCO, you normally have your more senior civilians rating them. Again, the real key though is if that individual is appointed by the commander as the supervisor and is listed as such on the rating scheme.

DUI Offense

Q: The After Action Review from the SFC selection board indicated that raters should mention a DUI offense on the NCO-ER. What is the right thing to do?

A: If an NCO receives a DUI, it should be specifically mentioned on the NCO-ER. You cannot mention any disciplinary action (such as article 15, letter of reprimand) but you can mention the offense that led to that action. Therefore, specifically stating the fact is acceptable and encouraged. For example:

o NCO exercised poor judgment by operating a motor vehicle while under the influence of alcohol

o NCO was cited for driving with blood alcohol content of 1.6 - well above the legal limit of .08

THE EVALUATOR

PSB Request a Copy of MMRB to Support Profile

Q: The local PSB keeps returning a NCO-ER on an NCO with a permanent profile because it did not have a copy of the MMRB results attached. Is this now required?

A: When an NCO has a profile, the rater will indicate such by entering PROFILE and the date of the profile in place of the APFT data. Additionally, a bullet comment is required that indicates whether the profile adversely affects duty performance. No other information or documents are required. A copy of the profile or the MMRB results are NOT required. The signatures of the rater and rated NCO on the NCO-ER are sufficient verification of accuracy. Further, there can be NO attachments to the NCO-ER when it is processed other than a reviewer's statement of non-concurrence or a memorandum of relief (when the relief for cause is directed by someone other than the rater or senior rater).

NCOER with Incorrect Correct Rating Chain

Q: I have been given an NCO-ER that does not reflect the correct rating officials. Should I sign it? If I refuse, what are my options? I also have some issues with the actual rating.

A: If there are some questions in your mind about the validity of the rating officials, you should raise that issue with your chain of command immediately. Your signature on the evaluation indicates that you agree that the rating officials are correct in accordance with the published rating scheme. If that is not the case, you need to get it resolved. If you have issues regarding the fairness/correctness of the actual evaluation, it is within your right to request - in writing - a commander's inquiry. If you request a commander's inquiry, the commander is then obligated (not a choice) to appoint an investigating officer (senior to the rating officials) to look into your allegations of injustice/unfairness. Once the investigating officer completes his report, he then forwards those findings back to the commander who will render a decision on the action, then forward the completed inquiry - with ALL attachments (sworn statements, etc.) to this office at DA PERSCOM, along with the original NCO-ER. The original NCO-ER is NOT to be processed until after the commander's inquiry is completed and then it is forwarded to this office, NOT to EREC. The correct/exact address is: Cdr, DA PERSCOM, ATTN: TAPC-MSE, 200 Stovall Street, Alexandria, VA 22332.

Suspension Pending Investigation (Relief for Cause)

Q: I have an NCO who is suspended pending formal investigation. He is charged with several things, including DUI. When should the Relief for Cause report be done?

A: The Relief for Cause report should be done AFTER the investigation is complete and the NCO is found guilty. If it is done before that and for some reason he is cleared (sometimes it happens on a technicality) then you will have to un-do everything you're done. Also, once he is found guilty of the charges, then you have certain, unquestionable bullets to use (clear, concise, accurate - always the key). Right now while he is on suspension, he gets no report until investigation is complete.

Using Quotas for Among the Best and 1/1 Ratings

Q: We have had several classes in my unit on writing NCO-ERs and one of the major issues coming out of one of the classes was the belief that only ONE soldier in a section or platoon could be rated 'Among the Best' and everyone else would have to be rated 'Fully Capable'. Same applies for the senior rater evaluations - only one can receive a '1/1' rating and everyone else falls behind that. Please clarify.

A: There is no such thing. There are no allocations or limitations on how many NCOs in a unit/platoon/section that are rated 'among the best' or given the top blocks in the senior rater's portion. Rating officials that implement such quotas are in violation of the intent of AR 623-205. This is not the OER system. Rating officials should always try to give their best ratings for the top NCOs but sometimes there are more than one NCO in a unit that absolutely stand out and may truly be 'among the best' and deserve '1/1' ratings in the senior rater blocks.

4 Digit Thru Date on the 2166-8

Q: With the implementation of the new NCO-ER form (DA 2166-8), it requires a 4-digit year in the FROM and THRU dates in Parts Ih. Does this also apply for the THRU date at the top of page two of the form; and what about the counseling and APFT dates?

A: The THRU date at the top of page two of DA 2166-8 will be entered with a 4-digit year. For example, November 2001 will be entered as 2001-11. However, there is NO CHANGE to the formats for counseling and APFT dates. You will continue to use the same format used on DA Form 2166-7.

Downloading the DA 2166-8 and 2166-8-1

Q: Where do I get the new NCO-ER Form?

A: The new forms (DA 2166-8 and 2166-8-1) are both available on the USAPA website (**www.usapa.army.mil**). If you experience difficulty downloading the form, send an email to the USAPA webmaster. Most problems encountered with downloading the forms are due to the version of formflow on the user's computer. If that is the case, the user must contact the local IMO to get the latest software installed to be able to download the new forms. According to the US Army Publishing Agency, they only release new forms using the latest version of the software so they cannot release it in different versions to accommodate those with out-dated systems or software. Also, there is an option at the USAPA site to download the latest version of the software from their site directly to your computer.

Being Assigned Below Your Rank

Q: I am a SSG who will be in the primary zone for promotion on the next SFC board. I recently arrived in my unit and was assigned to a SGT/E5 position although I informed my CSM that I am in the zone for SFC and was working in a SFC position at my last unit. He stated that the position I am assigned to does not matter but rather how the NCO-ER is written. Please advise. Will this hurt my chances for promotion?

A: According to regulation, you can be assigned one grade down or two grades up. Therefore, the position you are assigned to is within the regulatory guidelines. Your CSM is correct - the key factor is not where you are assigned on paper, but rather the actual duty you are performing and how that is articulated on the NCO-ER. Your performance and potential as reflected on your NCO-ER will have the greatest bearing on your selection for promotion.

Referencing An Allegation

Q: I am reviewing an NCO-ER where the rater made reference to an allegation on an informal investigation. Is this a legal comment?

A: In accordance with AR 623-205, paragraph s 6-5 and 6-6, no reference can be made to unverified derogatory information. An allegation in an information investigation is not verification of an offense - only if the NCO is charged and subsequently found guilty/liable. Rating officials may not reference investigations - ongoing or completed. However, they may mention misconduct that is verified and proven as a result of an investigation.

Can a Junior NCO's Rate an NCO of the Same Rank

Q: I have two sergeants first class and one of them was recently selected for promotion (on the newly released MSG list). The one that was not selected is senior to the SFC (P) by DOR. In view of their promotable status, can the junior NCO serve as the rater for the other one?

A: The quick answer is no. One of the fundamentals of the military is that seniority must be respected. As such, requests for junior NCOs to rate other NCOs who are senior to them by DOR are routinely disapproved. However, there is an exception. If the SFC (P) is serving in a valid E-8 position and is frocked they can then serve as the rater for the SFC. However, if both NCOs are serving in SFC positions, the junior NCO, regardless of him/her being promotable, cannot rate the senior SFC until such time as they pin on the MSG stripes and becomes senior by rank. Another unique situation is when a senior, non-promotable SFC is designated as rater to a SFC (P) **after** the SFC (P) was selected for promotion. It is clear that the SFC (P) will become senior as soon as the new stripes are pinned on so this rating change, although technically legal, is strongly discouraged and does not constitute good management practice.

Retirement and Transition leave NCOER's

Q: I have an NCO who is retiring and has requested an NCO-ER. He retires 1 August 2001 but his transition leave begins 1 May 2001. What would be the thru date of the report, April or July?

A: The thru date of the report would be April if he begins transition leave on 1 May. You do not extend reports to the actual retirement date if the NCO has actually departed the command on transition leave.

Profiles and APFT Scores

Q: I have a SGT on profile that was told he could get a 270 on the NCO-ER for his PT score. I told him that he was misinformed. Who's right?

A: You are right. There are provisions for soldiers who are E-4 and E-5 to have their scores averaged for promotion purposes only. It does not apply to NCO-ER. In the promotion arena, to qualify for promotion points, those soldiers with permanent physical profiles for the sit-up or push-up events will be granted 60 points for each event waived and use the actual score for each event taken; and must qualify on the two-mile run or approved alternate test according to FM 21-20. Soldiers taking an alternate event for the two-mile run attaining a 'GO,' will receive a score for that event average to the scores of the other two events. (This change was effective 1 Apr 95, is not retroactive and is applicable to promotion point calculations only.) Bottom line is on the NCO-ER the NCO receives a rating of "profile" if there is no PT run or alternate run event.

When a Rater is Relieved

Q: I have a 1SG whose company commander was relieved. The commander was his rater, since he is relieved the battalion commander did the rater and senior rater portion of the NCO-ER. Does the old rater's name go on the report and does the battalion commander sign in both places on the front in part II authentication?

A: The regulation states "when the rater is relieved, the senior rater will complete both the rater and senior rater portions of the report for each of the rater's subordinates, (provided minimum time qualifications are met)." Bottom line is the battalion commander's name goes in both places and he signs both as the rater and senior rater.

THE EVALUATOR

NCO's that Reenlist for the College Option How Are They Rated

Q: If a soldier reenlists for the college option, does that individual get a code 'S' for attending a civilian school? (**Please note:** these soldiers do make first formation and does PT with the unit. Also, if a person does not get a code for the college option, how is it justifiable to have someone attend school four to six months, get an NCO-ER for 12 or less months and accumulate anywhere from 18 to 20 plus credit hours when you're supposed to be working daily? The real question is will this affect the rated NCO?)

A: If an NCO is attending a civilian school, and during the period of attendance he is still responsible to the parent unit (such as formations and PT as you described), then the parent unit will continue to rate the individual and the period of attendance at school will be 'Rated.' If, on the other hand, the individual is completely released to attend school and is not responsible to the parent unit until school is completed, then the period will count as 'Non-Rated' time. In this event, a 'Change-of-Rater' report should be done before the individual begins school (just as you would for a PCS). Then when the individual returns from school, their rating period will begin anew and the time gone for school will be counted on the next evaluation report as 'Non-Rated.' For example, if the NCO departs for school on 26 August 2001 and their last report ended January 2001, they would get a 'Change of Rater' report in August and the dates would be 'from 01 02 thru 01 08' and the rated months would be '7.' Then, let's say they return from school in March 2002. They would be due an annual report in August 2002. That report would be 'from 01 09 thru 02 08' with '6' rated months and a non-rated code of 'S' for the other six months. There is no requirement that says individuals are rated solely for working daily. Even while attending school, if the NCO is responsible to the unit and rating officials, they can evaluate them in the various areas.

Can a Junior CSM Rate a Senior SGM

Q: Can a CSM rate a SGM who has more time-in-grade? I know that a CSM out-ranks a SGM based on position but according to the guidance in the regulation, the 1SG or CSM must be senior in pay grade or date of rank. It states nothing about position.

A: The CSM *cannot* rate a SGM unless he is senior by date of rank. There are exceptions to the policy but they must be requested in writing to DA PERSCOM (TAPC-MSE). As a general rule, we routinely disapprove such requests unless there are clearly special circumstances outlined in the request that are out of the ordinary.

Handwritten or Computer Generated "X"'s

Q: Regarding the digitized format of the NCO-ER, what is the official stance on whether or not the 'check boxes' are to be done by hand or via the application? In my last assignment, it was considered acceptable to check off the most qualified type boxes via the computer; in my current assignment this is permitted on OERs but not on NCO-ERs. If there's any guidance on this, I'd love to pass it along.

THE EVALUATOR

A: At one point, it was a requirement for the checks ('X') in the boxes in Part IVa-f and Parts Vc-d to be done by hand. However, that has now changed and they may be done either way - by hand or via the application. The only requirement is that they are consistent. If one 'X' is done by hand, then all must be done that way; or if one is typed, then all must be typed. This is spelled out in the revised regulation (AR 623-205).

Does the Word Potential Have to Appear in the Senior Rater's Comments

Q: I know that bullet comments are required by S/R (both performance and potential). My question is: does the word 'potential' have to be used as it relates to the soldier's potential? In the Jun 01 NCO-ER Update you listed examples of "Senior Rater Performance and Potential Bullets." In your examples, both performance and potential are addressed but the word 'potential' is not used. As a Bn CSM, I have had countless NCO-ERs returned for not having the word 'potential' in the S/R bullets block, Part Ve. Please advise.

A: The 'word' potential does not have to appear in the NCO-ER. The senior rater must address the NCO's potential but he/she does not have to use that specific word. For example, saying "promote now to master sergeant" addresses potential and would be sufficient if used.

Conditional Promotion to SGT & Then Administratively Reduced

Q: IAW AR 623-205, para 2-8a(4), NCOs reduced to CPL/SPC or below require a 'Change of Rater' NCO-ER. How does this affect a soldier who has been conditionally promoted to SGT and then administratively reduced?

A: No report is required for someone that was conditionally promoted and then administratively reduced for failing to meet the conditions.

Dating the Blocks on the NCOER

Q: Is there any regulatory or policy guidance on dating NCO-ERs? The MILPOs want the dates left blank. I say that we should be dating them when they are signed (just as we do for OERs).

A: The PSB (or MILPO) cannot dictate to rating officials on whether or not to date the NCO-ERs. A lot of PSBs ask for the dates to be left blank so they (the PSB folks) can ensure the dates are in sequence and not **before** the authorized signature date. However, as long as rating officials understand the rules for when they can be dated, it is always best for the rating officials to date the reports. The rule for dates on the NCO-ER is simple: for annual reports, they cannot be dated until the first day of the month following the end month of the report. For example, if the end month is June then the report cannot be signed/dated until 1 July, etc. The same applies for complete the record reports. For change of rater reports, they can be signed and dated anytime during the month in which the change occurs.

Proper Characters for MOS (O vs 0)

Q: I need your assistance in clarifying the sixth through ninth characters on NCO-ERs. I spoke with your predecessors in the past about the 5fifh character, and we all agreed that the fifth character should contain the letter "O" and not a zero. However, now the MILPO is starting to return NCO-ERs because the sixth through ninth characters are incorrect. In AR 614-200 it states the 6sixth and seventh characters should be "ZZ" if the soldier doesn't have an ASI and eighth and ninth characters should be "YY" if the soldiers aren't qualified in a language. Is there any new guidance pending, or what is correct?

A: AR 623-205 is the governing regulation for NCO-ERs. The sixth and seventh characters of the MOS are numbers (00) and the last two characters are letters (OO). For example, if an NCO (who's basic MOS is 11B4O) does **not** have an ASI or Language Identifier, then the nine-digit MOS is 11B4O**00OO**. Another example would be an NCO with an ASI but no language: 71L3O**E3OO**. One with no ASI but **does** have a language identifier: 75H5O**00SP**; lastly, one with both: 71L2O**F5FR**. You are correct about the fifth character of the MOS: it is a letter - therefore, if there is no SQI, then you use the letter "O." However, if there is no ASI or language identifier, only a five digit MOS is required on the NCO-ER so there is no real value or need in placing 00OO at the end of the PMOS.

Reviewer Has PCS'd Without Signing the Report

Q: I have a question on how to process an NCO-ER. We are getting guidance from the PSB that if the reviewer departs on PCS, we can't state that he is 'not available for signature.' The regulation isn't clear on this. What are my options?

A: There are no time limitations for the reviewer. If the original reviewer has PCS'd, then the replacement would be the reviewer. For example, if the rater is the company commander, and the senior rater is the battalion commander, and the reviewer is the Brigade Commander, and the Bde Cdr PCS's, then the new Bde Cdr would become the reviewer effective immediately and he/she can sign the report even if he/she has only been in the position for one Day. The 90 and 60 day limitations apply only to rater and senior rater.

THE EVALUATOR

What Score on the APFT Constitutes an Excellence

Q: What score on the APFT constitutes an excellence on the NCO-ER (overall score of 290 and above, 280 and above etc.)? Also, how many points must be scored in each event (90 or above, 80 or above, etc.) for an excellence on the NCO-ER?

A: The rule is 270 and above with at least 90 in each event. That qualifies for a physical fitness badge and an excellence bullet on the NCO-ER.

Comments Concerning Community Activities

Q: Can you give credit to soldiers that participate in or hold a position in community activities (that is not a command event) on the NCO-ER?

A: Absolutely!! Soldiers are always encouraged to actively participate in community events and it is most appropriate to indicate such on the NCO-ER. To further support this, the Army has the Military Outstanding Volunteer Service Medal that it awards to soldiers for their voluntary participation and contributions in the community.

Within Body Fat Standards Comment

Q: I have a soldier who needed to be taped to make the weight requirement (and yes, once taped he is within standards). He insists that the comment of "within body fat standards of AR 600-9" is *not* required anymore on the NCO-ER. I have done extensive follow up on this and the conclusion is the same, that the regulation did not change. However, many soldiers believe that there is a message "out there" that changes this requirement. Please advise.

A: Once a soldier meets the tape, the statement is **not** required on the NCO-ER anymore. That was put out in MILPER Message 98-044. It will be included in the new regulation when it is released this fall. In the meantime, if the soldier meets body fat standards, you cannot state it on the NCO-ER anymore. You just indicate the NCO's HT/WT and 'YES.'

NCO That is Overweight, Does not Meet Body Fat Standards but has a Medical Condition

Q: I have an NCO who currently has a profile which prohibits him from taking the APFT. The problem is he is over the weight screening table and does not meet the body fat standards. The NCO-ER indicates 72/232 'NO' and a bullet comment indicating that a doctor has evaluated weight as medical disorder and treatment is pending. The rater checked the 'success' box. The unit has not put the soldier in a weight control program due to the medical condition and states they will *not* mark 'Needs Improvement.' Is the bullet comment acceptable and can the NCO be rated as 'success?'

THE EVALUATOR

A: The correct entry is '72/232 NO.' The bullet should state something to the effect as the following:

> o soldier has a confirmed medical disorder which resulted in the overweight condition; soldier is not currently enrolled in an overweight program due to medical diagnosis

As far as whether to check 'SUCCESS' or 'NEEDS IMPROVEMENT,' that is the rater's call. If the rater feels strongly that the *only* reason for the overweight is the medical condition, then he may elect to check 'SUCCESS.' However, the 'NO' must remain in the top portion with the bullet comment explaining it.

NCO Fails APFT and Get a Profile Preventing a Retest

Q: An NCO took an APFT in Jan 01 and failed. Before the 90 day window was up for the retest, the soldier received a profile (Apr 01) preventing the retest. The recovery period for the profile extended beyond the end date of end of the NCO-ER. Should the entry in Part IVc be 'FAIL' with comment that says something to the effect "Soldier unable to retake failed APFT due to profile" or should it read 'PROFILE?'

A: Unfortunately for the NCO, you must report 'FAIL' since that is the latest report he has on file and it was within the past 12 months. However, you should also indicate in the remarks that he was unable to take the retest due to temporary profile. The entry would be something like this:

> FAIL 0101 HT/WT Yes (or NO)

> o soldier failed the 2-mile run event on the APFT; did not retest yet due to temporary profile (you must indicate what event(s) he failed)

Bullets Past or Present Tense

Q: Should the bullet comments on NCO-ERs be past tense or present tense?

A: They should be past tense since you are rating the NCO for a period that has now passed. However, some raters still use present tense in their writing. The reports will still be processed as long as the bullets are consistent. However, the correct way is past tense.

Can a SFC rate a SSG in an SFC Position

Q: Can a SFC serving as the Maintenance Control Supervisor rate a SSG serving in a SFC position as Section Chief?

A: Yes. A SFC is senior to a SSG by rank and therefore can serve as rater for any SSG under his supervision regardless of the positions they occupy.

THE EVALUATOR

MSG rating a GS-13

Q: Where do I look to find rank equivalents or levels between civilians and soldiers? Can a MSG rate a GS-13, or Senior Rate the soldiers under the GS-13?

A: This is an absolute no-go. A MSG may NOT senior rate soldiers rated by a GS-13. A GS-13 is equivalent to a Major/04 so obviously, should not be rated by a MSG (or a SGM for that matter). (See Figure 3-1, AR 623-105, OER Regulation). Even if you had a SGM there, soldiers that are rated by the GS-13, should NOT be senior rated by the SGM unless that SGM is the actual RATER of the GS-13 (which is not likely the case). I DO realize that there are some unique and special situations across the Army - especially in remote sites; but the rating guidelines and limitations must be adhered to. Any exceptions to this must be requested in writing and approved by this office.

Soldier on Profile and Unable to take APFT

Q: I have a soldier that is on a profile and the ending period of her NCO-ER is 31 August 2001. She was on profile due to surgery and was unable to take the PT test before 31 Aug 01. IAW AR 623-205, a statement must be given if you put PROFILE in the block. Does this still stand?

A: Yes, the 'profile' statement is still required if the soldier could not take the APFT. Many folks use the generic statement such as: o *profile does not hinder duty performance...* While this is acceptable, it is better to be more specific. This is especially true if it is just a temporary condition: o *temporary profile does not hinder duty performance - soldier is dedicated to overcoming condition.*

P3 Profile Prohibits taking the APFT

Q: I am reviewing an NCO-ER on an individual who has a P3 profile. One of the bullets state the following: *P-3 profile prohibited an APFT during this rating period.* Can this bullet comment be used or should it state *profile does not hinder duty performance*?

A: Statement may **not** read *P3 profile prevented taking the APFT.* It must address whether or not it affects ***duty performance***, NOT the ability to take the APFT. Therefore, the statement should read: **o P3 profile does (or does not) hinder duty performance.** However, if the rater says it DOES hinder duty performance, then he needs to be specific and indicate what duties the soldier cannot do. For example: **o due to physical profile, soldier was unable to deploy to Bosnia to serve as broadcast journalist.**

THE EVALUATOR

NCO in the Overweight Program Does not Meet Body Fat Standards but is Making Progress

Q: One of the NCO's in the unit is enrolled in the weight control program because he exceeds the body fat standards. However, he is making great progress in the program and the rater wants to rate him "success" as opposed to "needs improvement". Can you give a "success" rating with a "no" entry for HT/WT?

A: It is the rater's call. The regulation does not **mandate** a 'needs improvement' rating with a 'no' entry. The short answer is **YES**, the rater can rate the NCO as "success". *However*, the rater should be cautioned to be consistent across the board when rating other NCOs in similar situations. As long as another NCO, who is also making good progress in the program is rated with a 'success' by this rater, then there are no concerns. Also, keep in mind that success normally means the NCO meets minimum standards. Although an individual is making satisfactory progress in the weight control program, the fact that he/she still has not reached minimum ht/wt or body fat standards, automatically sends the message that this is an area where he/she needs to improve. Rating officials should look closely and carefully at this and ensure the message you send is clear and intentional. *It's your call.*

Comments Concerning Areas of Special Emphasis or Appointed Duties

Q: If 'Areas of Special Emphasis' and 'Appointed Duties' are listed on the front of the NCO-ER, (Parts III d and e), is there a requirement to address them on the back of the NCO-ER?

A: AR 623-205 does not require raters to address areas or duties listed in Parts III d & e. However, it stands to reason that if there are areas of special emphasis and/or appointed duties which are important enough to list in Parts III d & e, then they should be equally important enough to warrant a bullet comment. This is the only way those reviewing the report can get a clear picture of how well the NCO performed in those special emphasis areas or with the additional duties. The idea is to give the NCO credit for performing well with the extra requirements.

Commander's Inquiry

Paragraph 2-15, AR 623-205 provides guidance and information on the conduct, preparation and submission of commander's inquiries. Its purpose is to investigate allegations of unjust or illegal evaluation reports when requested by subordinates, **before** a report is submitted for filing in the NCO's Official Military Personnel File (OMPF). Normally, the issue is raised by the rated NCO. However, anyone having knowledge of the alleged illegality or injustice may bring it to the attention of the commander. By regulation, the inquiry will be conducted by a major or above who is in the rating chain above the rating officials. In order for the commander's inquiry to be fully successful and meet its intended purpose, (prevent injustice to the NCO and/or correct errors), the commander must get involved early and ensure prompt action before the report is processed. A large number of the cases we receive involve reports that have already been forwarded through the PSB to EREC for final processing. It then becomes a much longer and more involved process to correct errors once the report is already on the system. Once a soldier formally requests a commander's inquiry, NCO-ER processing on that report should cease until the inquiry is conducted and completed.

CLARIFICATION OF CHANGES

Instead of the usual questions and answers, space in this edition will be devoted to clarifying issues regarding the new NCO-ER forms and the changes in the upcoming regulation. Widest dissemination is strongly encouraged.

--DA Form 2166-8 requires a **4-digit year** in the FROM and THRU dates on the front and in the THRU date on the back of the form. Those dates should now be entered as 2002 (instead of just '02'). There are no other changes in date formats on the form. Therefore, the date of rank, counseling dates and APFT date will all be entered in the same format as they always were.

--The rated **NCO's signature on the NCO-ER certifies the following**: he has seen the completed report (except the reviewer's signature and check mark); the administrative data, APFT data, height/weight data; and counseling dates are correct; and the rating officials are correct (based on the rating scheme). The signature does NOT mean the rated NCO agrees with the evaluation. Therefore, NCOs should not refuse to sign the report unless there is some incorrect data in one or more of the areas just mentioned.

--**Part IVa** (Army Values) has been **changed** on the 2166-8 to **reflect the current Army values**. Bullet comments are 'required' for any 'NO' check marks in this area. Comments are 'optional' for 'YES' marks. However, rating officials should comment on any of the Army values that are particularly strong and stand out about the rated NCO.

--**Bullet comments** must be **preceded by a small o**. That has not changed. However, in the revised regulation, we clarified the format for the bullets. They are not sentences so therefore should not be capitalized at the beginning and should not have punctuation at the end. For example, a proper bullet comment would look this way: o awarded the physical fitness badge

--**Bullet comments should be worded in 'past' tense** since they reflect accomplishments /contributions that have already been completed. The exception is when the rating official is addressing values (which are on-going).

--Under new procedures, the actual **APFT score is not required to justify excellence** in the APFT area. As long as the NCO **scored 270 on the APFT with at least 90 in each event**, then the rater only needs to enter the statement "awarded physical fitness badge". This does NOT preclude the rater from entering the APFT score in an instance where the NCO scored 300 on the APFT and the rater just wants to highlight that fact. Bottom line is: score is not required but is not forbidden. Score 'is' still required when a soldier fails the APFT.

--The semi-annual APFT is administered twice a year. When time for the NCO-ER arrives, the **latest APFT date must be used** - no exceptions. **However**, in instances where an NCO did not take an APFT during the most recent administration, the **previous APFT date should be used as long as it was within the last year. For NCO-ER purposes, APFT dates and scores are considered valid and current as long as they are not older than 12 months.**

--When the new regulation is released, **two additional reports** will be authorized for the first time. **One is the 'senior rater option'**; this report allows senior raters who are leaving, to render reports on NCOs they senior rater. This is an optional report and not mandatory. However, in instances where the senior rater is changing and the rated NCO will be due a report no more than 60 days later, the senior rater should exercise this option. This will preclude the rated NCO from receiving a report with just 'rater' input (due to lack of qualification time by the new senior rater). The other report that's newly authorized is the **'60-day short tour option' report.** This is used only in designated short tour areas (14 months or less) where the rated NCO has at least 60 but less than 90 rated days under the rater's supervision. This allows NCOs who are deployed for short periods or when personnel turnover is frequently high, to receive evaluation reports due to the exceptional circumstances. Again, this is an 'optional' report and although initiated by the rater, the senior rater may disapprove it.

--**Complete the record NCO-ERs will only require '90' rated days**, as opposed to six months under the old procedures. This change does not affect the MSG/E8 selection board which convenes in February 2002, but will affect subsequent boards.

SIGNATURE DATES

The signature dates on the NCO-ER have become a major point of contention in recent months. Some rating officials contend that the local PSBs will not accept reports if they are already dated. The regulatory guidance is simple. The report should be dated when the rating officials sign the report, provided it is after the end date of the report. For example, 'Annual' and 'Complete-the- Record' reports may not be dated prior to the 1st day of the month after the report end date. Therefore, a report ending in November should be dated 1 December or later. Also, all four dates should either be the same or dated in sequence: the rater signs before the senior rater; senior rater signs before the rated NCO; rated NCO signs before the reviewer. It is the rating officials' responsibility to date the reports as they are signed and local PSBs should not reject them unless they are incorrectly dated (out of sequence or before the THRU date ends). Note that 'Change of Rater' and 'Relief for Cause' reports may be signed anytime during the month the event occurs.

THE EVALUATOR

NCOs PERFORMING DUTY IN OFFICER POSITIONS

If an NCO is assigned to an officer position on the MTOE or TDA, the appropriate duty title may be reflected on the NCO-ER. However, the DMOS that is reflected on the NCO-ER (Part IIIb) is the ENLISTED MOS that most closely relates to the particular specialty. The rater may reflect the scope of responsibility in the actual duty description.

EXCELLENCE RATINGS FOR PHYSICAL FITNESS/MILITARY BEARING

There has been considerable concern regarding flexibility in rendering 'excellence' verses 'success' ratings in Part IVc on the NCO-ER. The regulatory guidance dictates that excellence based 'solely' on APFT score requires at least 90 in each of the three events and a minimum total score of 270. However, raters still have the option of rating excellence in this area when the APFT score is less than 270 provided the bullet comments are strong enough to support such a rating. The biggest issue seems to concern NCOs who score above 90 in the push-up and sit-up events but takes an alternate aerobic event. One example cited an NCO who scored 95 and 92 points respectively in the push-up and sit-up events and completed the 2 1/2 mile walk nearly 5 minutes below the time limit. Obviously that individual is physically fit and has made fitness a personal priority. That, combined with his military bearing and mental toughness, *'could'* qualify him for a rating of excellence if the rater deems it justifiable. Again, this is not mandated by the NCO-ER regulation and is at the discretion of the rating official based on his best judgment.

SENIOR RATER COMMENTS ON POTENTIAL

It is mandatory that senior raters address 'potential' in Part Ve on the NCO-ER. However, potential involves more than just promotion. It also includes schools and assignment considerations. One rating official raised the issue that he rates a newly promoted SGT/E5 that is not yet eligible for promotion to Staff Sergeant and even when he is eligible, going before the board and getting promoted is more a personal effort. In such an instance, the senior rater can still address long-term potential, which looks 3-5 years down the road. For example, if it is a hard-charging NCO with great initiative, the senior rater may state that he *possesses definite potential for rapid advancement to the senior NCO level.* The point here is that the senior rater is not limited to just addressing potential for advancement to the next grade, but also *long-term* potential as well as types of assignments and schools.

WEBSITE GUIDANCE - OFFICIAL OR UNOFFICIAL

There have been questions regarding the validity of information/guidance contained on the NCO-ER website. For all concerned, the NCO-ER regulation (AR 623-205) contains specific guidance, policies, and procedures. However, over time, there are often areas that need clarification or elaboration. Obviously we can not publish a new regulation every time there is a policy issue that requires clarification so it is easier to provide that information via the website. In exceptional cases where the issue is widespread, we may use the MILPER message as the forum for clarifying issues. However, as a general rule the website is used and since it is an official website, any information contained there may be considered the 'official' DA PERSCOM position on NCO-ER related issues. Anytime there is a doubt or question on an issue, call or email the NCO-ER Policy office for clarification. Official policy guidance is issued everyday via email and telephone so the regulation is not a sole source document for official guidance.

CHAPTER 7

WORD LISTING

**Note: The following word list was designed to address items of
excellence, success, and needs improvement**

THE EVALUATOR

Word Listing

Adjectives

Abandoned: deserted, forsaken, discarded, relinquished, rejected

Abject: hopeless, pitiful, deplorable, terrible, lacking

Able: capable, efficient, competent, skillful, clever, gifted, proficient, expert, highly qualified, accomplished

Abominable: despicable, reprehensible, hateful, revolting, vile, foul

Aboveboard: candid, open, honest, frank, sincere, truthful, straight-shooting

Abrupt: sudden, unexpected, unanticipated, quick, hasty, swift

Absolute: unrestricted, unrestrained, unlimited, unconditional, unqualified, unbounded, complete, supreme, pure, full, conclusive

Absurd: unreasonable, illogical, irrational, foolish, senseless

Abundant: ample, sufficient, enough, plenty, bountiful, rich, lavish

Abusive: harsh, mean, insulting, offensive, cruel

Academic: school, educational, studious, learned, educated, theoretical

Accessible: available, ready, reachable, approachable

Accomplished: cultivated, learned, finished, existing, achievement, realization, proven, masterly, polished, talented, gifted, brilliant

Accountable: liable, answerable, responsible, culpable

Accurate: correct, faithful, true, faithfulness

Active: energetic, vigorous, spirited, ambitious, forceful, aggressive, zealous

Acute: sagacious, astute, shrewd, discerning, keen, sharp

Adaptable: flexible, open-minded, accommodating, amenable

Additional: extra, spare, supplementary

Adequate: suitable, tolerable, fitting, ample, enough

Administrative: execution, management, distribution, leadership

Admissible: permitted, allowed, legitimate

Advantageous: helpful, beneficial, useful, favorable, win-win

Adverse: unfavorable, contrary, opposing, hostile, unfriendly

Aggressive: energetic, assertive, hostile, belligerent, combative

Agile: nimble, limber, dexterous, quick, swift, clever, alert, keen

Aimless: directionless, undirected, unorganized, erratic, pointless, unfocused, unpredictable, random

Alert: aware, attentive, observant, lively, perceptive, watchful, sharp

Allied: joint, combined, united, associated, affiliated

Apathetic: indifferent, unresponsive, impassive, unconcerned

Apparent: evident, obvious, open, overt, blatant

Applicable: relevant, adaptable, fitting, useful, suitable

Approximate: rough, estimated, roughly

Arduous: difficult, hard, exhausting, tiring

Argumentative: quarrelsome, combative

Arrogant: overbearing, vain, conceited, egotistical

Articulate: intelligible, meaningful, expressive, eloquent

Assertive: positive, forceful, decisive, strong-willed, confident

Astute: shrewd, quick, bright, acute, smart

Athletic: strong, powerful, robust

Authoritarian: inflexible, strict, harsh, dogmatic, disciplinary, uncompromising, severe, unyielding

Awkward: clumsy, uncoordinated, unskillful, difficult, inept

Balanced: fair, equitable, just, impartial

Blunt: frank, candid, outspoken, tactless, insensitive

Brave: courageous, valorous, heroic, fearless, undaunted

Brilliant: distinguished, illustrious, clever, keen, intelligent, brainy, wise

Calculating: scheming, plotting, manipulative, contriving

Callow: immature, inexperienced, unseasoned, untried, uninformed, ignorant

Calm: smooth, quiet, still, unshaken, cool, composed

Capable: proficient, competent, qualified, able, talented, effective, skilled

Careful: cautious, watchful, observant, attentive, prudent, meticulous

Careless: thoughtless, mindless, rash, sloppy, inconsiderate

Clandestine: covert, private, concealed

THE EVALUATOR

Commendable: praiseworthy, worthy, admirable, honorable, creditable, notable, deserving

Competent: qualified, able, fit, efficient, capable, skilled, expert

Confident: certain, sure, positive, assured

Contagious: catching, infectious, transmittable

Corrupt: dishonest, shady, unscrupulous, unethical, immoral

Cowardly: timid, apprehensive, fearful

Culpable: guilty, liable

Debatable: questionable, doubtful, unsure, uncertain

Deceitful: insincere, untrustworthy, false, deceptive

Decided: certain, unmistakable, definite

Decisive: conclusive, indisputable, final

Defiant: rebellious, disobedient

Deliberate: intentional, planned, prearranged, willful, voluntary, calculated

Determined: resolute, resolved, decided, firm

Diligent: hard-working, untiring, thorough

Disgruntled: displeased, irritated, dissatisfied

Disheveled: unkempt, disorderly, sloppy, messy, untidy

Disobedient: insubordinate, rebellious, defiant, noncompliant

Disrespectful: rude, impolite

Distinguished: celebrated, famous, illustrious, renowned, noted

Devoted: eager, loyal, faithful

Eager: zealous, earnest

Effective: adequate, effectual, efficient, capable, operative

Efficient: effective, productive, capable, competent

Elaborate: complex, involved, complicated

Elite: best, select

Essential: needed, crucial, vital, key, important

Exceptional: extraordinary, uncommon, rare, unusual, superior

Expert: proficient, skilled

Faithful: loyal, devoted, constant, steadfast, reliable, dependable

THE EVALUATOR

Fatal: terminal, deadly, lethal

Formidable: awesome, imposing, impressive, overpowering

Forceful: strong, commanding

Illustrious: distinguished, eminent, renowned

Inappropriate: unsuited, improper, unbecoming

Incapable: unskilled, inept, incompetent, unfit, unqualified, untrained, inadequate, ineffective

Inexhaustible: unfailing, unlimited

Inordinate: excessive, lavish, undue, unreasonable

Invaluable: priceless, precious, rare

Judicious: sensible, wise, just, tactful, prudent

Marked: conspicuous, prominent, noticeable, distinct

Meritorious: commendable, noteworthy, exceptional, laudable

Meticulous: exact, careful, precise, perfectionist

Misappropriate: misuse, embezzle, abuse

Misconduct: dereliction, impropriety

Neglectful: negligent, careless, remiss, inattentive, derelict

Outstanding: eminent, prominent, signal

Paramount: supreme, chief, dominant

Peculiar: particular, individual, distinctive, typical, unique, exclusive, specific

Perfect: exact, accurate, precise, true, correct, flawless, faultless, complete

Popular: accepted, preferred, approved, sought after

Possessing: possessed of, master of, in possession of, endowed with, owning, mastering

Practical: useful, sensible, realistic, down-to-earth

Prestigious: distinguished, illustrious, honored, respected, famous

Qualified: experienced, trained, competent, suited, able, adept, skilled

Relevant: related, pertinent, connected, associated

Reliable: dependable, faithful, trustworthy, responsible, conscientious

Sensational: outstanding, spectacular, extraordinary, exceptional, exciting

Sensible: sound, intelligent, wise, prudent, reasonable, credible

Simultaneous: accompanying, concurrent, coexisting

THE EVALUATOR

Stipulate: specify, insist

Stringent: strict, demanding, rigorous, exacting

Unequaled: unmatched, unparalleled, incomparable, inimitable, unique

Undeniable: unquestionable, incontestable, certain, sure, conclusive, absolute

Unparalleled: peerless, unrivaled, inimitable, unique

Verbs

Abandon	Abolish	Absorb	Abuse
Accept	Acclaim	Accommodate	Accomplish
Achieve	Acknowledge	Acquire	Adapt
Admonish	Advance	Advise	Advocate
Affect	Affirm	Alleviate	Analyze
Appoint	Assemble	Assess	Assumed
Avoid	Befit	Benefit	Berate
Broach	Certify	Challenge	Combine
Communicate	Compete	Comply	Condone
Conceive	Consent	Conserve	Consult
Consolidated	Constitute	Coordinate	Correlate
Corroborate	Crack	Delegate	Demonstrate
Disappoint	Disapprove	Disclose	Discredit
Distinguish	Dominate	Earn	Educate
Embellish	Emerge	Emit	Encourage
Engineered	Enhance	Enlighten	Establish
Evaluate	Evolve	Exchange	Execute
Exemplify	Exempt	Exhibit	Expect
Facilitate	Familiarize	Fulfill	Formulate
Generate	Illuminate	Impartial	Implemented
Impress	Improvised	Inaugurate	Initiate

THE EVALUATOR

Inspire	Instill	Interpret	Manage
Motivate	Persevere	Justify	Kindle
Lag	Liquidate	Manage	Mention
Misinform	Misjudge	Mismanage	Negate
Neglect	Negotiate	Neutralize	Officiate
Persist	Pioneered	Portray	Possess
Probe	Procure	Rationalize	Realize
Renovate	Reorganize	Restore	Seize
Signify	Strengthen	Stimulate	Stipulate
Strive	Subdue	Supervise	Surpass
Teach	Transform	Underestimate	Vacate

Nouns

Ability: talent, capacity, faculty, aptitude, skill

Acclamation: ovation, acclaim

Accolade: award, honor, tribute, prize, praise, compliment

Accomplishment: achievement, attainment, realization, performance

Acknowledgment: recognition, credit, affirmation

Admonition: reprimand, reproach, rebuke, warning

Adoration: worship, devotion, honor

Advocacy: championship, support, patronage, supporting, backing, recommendation

Alternative: choice, option, substitute

Ambition: drive, desire, zeal, push, striving, aspiration, goal, objective, purpose

Appraisal: evaluation, judgment, estimate, assessment, valuation

Appreciation: gratitude, grateful

Aptitude: ability, capacity, capability, talent, genius

Authority: command, control, power

Bearing: conduct, comportment, manner, demeanor, behavior

Brilliance: brightness, luster, glow, shine, splendor, intelligence, wisdom, inventiveness, ingenuity, quickness, sharpness, excellence

THE EVALUATOR

Candidate: applicant, nominee, competitor, contender

Candor: frankness, openness, honesty, truthfulness, bluntness

Casualty: injured, victim, wounded, fatality

Catastrophe: disaster, misfortune, tragedy, havoc

Collaborator: associate, confederate, teammate, coworker, partner

Combatant: soldier, service member, warrior, fighter

Competence: ability, capability, efficient, skill, proficiency, expertise

Concealment: hide, cover, disguise, mask, shield, cloak, camouflage

Consequence: result, outcome, development

Consideration: thought, attention, notice, heed, contemplation, reflection

Contribution: donation, gift, grant, offering, charity, alms

Decision: conclusion, judgment, verdict, resolution, result

Dedication: devotion, steadfastness

Demeanor: conduct, behavior, manner, bearing, presence

Deficiency: shortage, insufficiency, inadequacy, flaw, defect, weakness

Determination: resoluteness, decision, firmness

Diplomacy: tact, finesse, discretion, prudence

Egress: depart, exit, withdraw, escape, discharge

Effectiveness: productive

Endurance: stamina, durability, strength, persistence

Equality: justice, fairness, evenness, balance

Esprit de corps: team spirit, group unity, camaraderie, group pride

Ethics: moral, decent, honorable, right, proper, just, fair

Excellence: merit, superiority, greatness, worth, perfection

Expertise: special skill, specialization, professionalism

Fortitude: endurance, courage, guts, determination, bravery, intrepidity, heroism, valor

Half-hearted: lackluster, faint, unenthusiastic, indifferent, apathetic

Hindrance: block, obstacle, obstruction, interference, constraint, barrier

Idea: concept, thought, insight, interpretation, notion, inspiration

Imagination: inventiveness, creativity, resourcefulness, ingenuity

Implement: begin, activate, start

THE EVALUATOR

Information: data, knowledge, evidence

Initiative: lead, originality, creativity, motivation

Inspiration: motive, encouragement, thought, idea

Integration: assimilation, combination, blending, mixing, union

Integrity: virtue, purity, honesty, decency

Loyalty: devotion, faithfulness, allegiance

Mainstay: anchor, backbone, pillar, principal, foundation

Maintenance: repair, upkeep, protection

Mandate: decree, command, order, directive

Mentor: adviser, counselor, teacher, tutor, guru

Misappropriate: misuse, steal, embezzle, defraud

Misconduct: dereliction, misbehavior, transgression

Motive: reason, motivation, intention, purpose, object, cause, rationale

Nurture: maintain, strengthen, sustain, tend, prepare, discipline, train, cultivate, educate

Obligation: responsibility, debt, duty, liability

Patience: endurance, tolerance, calm

Plan: idea, proposal, scheme, suggestion

Rapport: relationship, affiliation, fellowship, connection

Reliance: confidence, trust, faith, assurance

Skill: dexterity, adroitness, proficiency, cleverness, faculty, aptitude

Tactful: diplomatic, smooth, considerate, thoughtful

Talent: ability, cleverness, faculty, gift, aptitude

Understanding: insight, perception, comprehension, discernment

Willful: deliberate, intended, planned

Willingness: desire, readiness, eagerness, enthusiasm